I0112001

# IRON SKILLET MAN

## A COOKBOOK AND PARODY

by Hallee Bridgeman

a.k.a. "Hallee the Homemaker™"

THE STARK TRUTH ABOUT PEPPER AND POTS

Published by
House of Bread Books™

**H+B HOUSE OF BREAD™**

PUBLISHED BY: House of Bread Books™*, an imprint of Olivia Kimbrell Press™, P.O. Box 4393, Winchester, KY 40392-4393

The House of Bread Books™ colophon and logo are trademarks of Olivia Kimbrell Press™.

*Olivia Kimbrell Press™ is a publisher offering true to life, meaningful fiction and relevant nonfiction from a Christian worldview intended to uplift the heart and engage the mind. For more information about the mission of House of Bread Books™, refer to our mission statement at the back of this book.

Library Cataloging Data
Bridgeman, Hallee (Hallee A. Bridgeman) 1972-
  Iron Skillet Man; the Stark Truth About Pepper and Pots/ Hallee Bridgeman
    262 p. 23cm x 15cm (9in x 6 in.)
Summary: Book 3 in Hallee's Galley parody cookbook series tangles with the cultural obsession with super powered heroes and villains while serving up delicious recipes.
  ISBN: 978-1-939603-32-6 (trade perfect)  ISBN-10: 1-939603-32-3
1. real food 2. whole food 3. artisan cooking 4. natural living 5. parody 6. satire 7. recipes
  Library of Congress Control Number 2014904592
  [Non-Fic.] 613-DC22

# IRON SKILLET MAN

## A COOKBOOK AND PARODY

by Hallee Bridgeman

a.k.a. "Hallee the Homemaker™"

Hallee's Galley book 3

# "In brightest day or blackest night, no recipe shall escape my skillet!"

## Rave Reviews for Iron Skillet Man:

**"My *skillet* skills were *cast* into real peril.
Iron Skillet Man came to the rescue!"**
We're sure the **DAILY MIRROR** wishes they had quoted this

**"I was a child with heavy metal until I discovered
this cookbook. Then, 'Shazaam!' Marvelous magical
meals in minutes!"**
**THE TIMES** this has been said are numerous

**"Thanks to this cookbook I finally learned
what astronauts have for breakfast.
Unidentified *Frying* Objects!"**
Part of **SOUTHERN LIVING** is overhearing these kinds of remarks
now and then

**"I finally learned the stark truth about
pepper and pots."**
A homemaker in the **USA TODAY** said

# Table of Contents!

## HOW TO READ THIS COOKBOOK

You will find symbols at the top of each recipe to help you better use and navigate this cookbook. Here is a key (legend) to assist you in interpreting them.

❄ Freezes well

Sometimes, it's nice to pre-make something, or make big batches and freeze the quantity you'll need. You can just pull a container out of the freezer and gravy is ready to go when you need it. For the broths and stocks, I freeze in 1-cup increments. For gravies, freeze and reheat to 165° degrees F (75° degrees C), whisking it smooth.

⏱ Quick and Easy

Some nights or mornings, quick and easy is the theme of the meal. These dishes take little preparation and use supplies that don't take a lot of planning or cooking times.

✝ Lent/Daniel Fast/Vegan Friendly

These dishes are 100% real whole food, vegan friendly. No meat products, no meat, no dairy or egg, no processed foods. Suitable for a Daniel Fast, Lent, or incorporating into a vegan menu.

🫘 Vegetarian

Not "vegan" – may contain dairy products or egg, but no meat.

✡ Kosher Friendly

If you keep Kosher, your kitchen is Kosher, and your ingredients are Kosher, these dishes are Kosher friendly. No dairy mixing with meat, no unclean meats, etc.

## Holiday Fare

This dish goes well with a roast turkey, rack of lamb, goose, or a roast beef: traditional holiday meals.

## Gluten Free

All ingredients in this recipe are gluten free.

## International

A recipe that is a traditional dish in a country other than the United States.

## Calls for alcohol

This recipe originally calls for alcohol, usually wine. If you abstain from alcohol even in cooking, you can substitute a 100% pure white or dark grape juice (make sure there is no apple juice in it) along with one tsp of distilled vinegar to approximate the same flavor and properties while cooking but without the alcohol. Substitutes are always noted in the recipes.

## Crock Pot

Either can be or should be prepared in a crock pot. It's wonderful to have a dish you can leave cooking on its own while you do your day.

## Entrée

This is not just a side dish - it is a full entrée.

Other symbols used in this cookbook:

## More information on the world wide web

When you can find more information about something on the internet, I have put an INFORMATION symbol ⓘ next to it and provided the link address in the notes.

## FOREWORD UNTO DAWN

For years now I have been preparing recipes for the Hallee the Homemaker™ blog with the intent of publishing a cookbook. In all those years of preparing myself, until very recently, I never imagined I would create the "Parody Series" of cookbooks. But, honestly, once I came up with *50 Shades of Gravy*, and followed that with *The Walking Bread*, I find myself unable to stop coming up with parody titles for fun cookbooks.

Welcome to Hallee's Galley book number 3: *Iron Skillet Man*.

I love skillet meals. I think they're just super. I have a set of cast iron skillets that are my go-to for so many recipes. Good, seasoned cast iron is such an amazing cooking tool because of the way it distributes the heat from the stove (or in the cases of some of the recipes in this book, the grill, oven, or campfire) with a safe, nonstick coating.

If you take care of your cast iron properly, it will last a lifetime and even longer. It can literally last for generations. I know this because one of my favorite cast iron skillets belonged to my great-grandmother.

I also have a deep stainless steel skillet that I use as often as possible. If you've read my Hallee the Homemaker™ blog, you'll have seen that skillet in countless recipe photographs.

I make all kinds of things in my skillets – from casseroles to sauces to gravies to breads to cakes. This cookbook is chock full of recipes – some you wouldn't even think of cooking in a skillet. I hope you enjoy these recipes as much as my family does.

## THE STARK TRUTH ABOUT PEPPER AND POTS

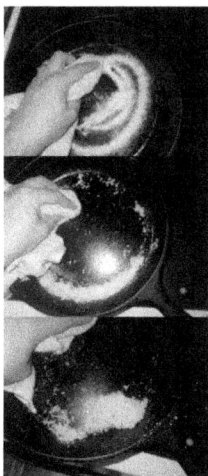

The best way to clean a cast iron skillet is with coarse salt.

Never use pepper to clean your cast iron pots.

The stark truth is this – pepper won't clean cast iron. There you have it.

So what's the answer? Just pour some coarse salt into the skillet and use a sturdy towel to scrub. You want to use Kosher salt or sea salt if possible. I even use salt after frying fish, and when I'm done, there isn't even a slight odor remaining. After you scrub it clean, just wipe the salt out, lightly oil the pan like above, and store it.

Another option is to cut a potato into circles or wedges and use that to scrub the salt into the skillet. This is especially helpful if your skillet shows any signs of rust.

Try never to clean seasoned cast iron with modern dish soaps or detergents. It can strip away the "seasoning" that coats the iron and protects the metal – which will cause it to rust.

Try never to let your seasoned cast iron "soak" because that will certainly cause it to rust, even if it is well seasoned.

If you must get your cast iron wet to help clean it, then go ahead but dry it immediately by first toweling it completely dry then placing it on a hot stove or in a hot oven. Once dry, just coat a paper towel with oil (grapeseed oil or cold pressed organic flaxseed oil) and wipe down the skillet then let it sit on a hot burner or in the oven so that the pores of the cast iron will soak up oil not water.

ⓘ For more good information about cleaning cast iron with pictures, visit my blog:
http://www.halleethehomemaker.com/cleaning-cast-iron

## THE FINAL WORD ON SEASONING CAST IRON

There is almost nothing better for cooking even complex meals than a well seasoned cast-iron skillet. The only thing that cooks more evenly, in my opinion, is a stainless steel skillet, though in my opinion cast iron is better suited for certain dishes. For example, when searing, say, Ahi Tuna or any red meat. In fact, I prefer the cast iron for cooking red meats. For one thing, it moves effortlessly from a stove top to an oven or a grill to a stove top.

> Before using your cast iron skillet or cast iron cookware for the first time, you want to season it. It's a lot easier than it sounds.

Seasoned cast iron is also a perfectly safe nonstick surface. Studies have shown that many mass produced "nonstick" surfaces such as Teflon® are actually toxic. So the important things to know about cast iron is how to season it, how to repair it if needed, and how to maintain it once seasoned. To that end, there are three really important factors you need to understand to perfectly season your cast iron.

**1) You must use the right oil**

**2) Strip for success**

**3) Seasoning is different than cooking**

This section is going to explain, to the very best of my ability, those three things. I sincerely hope that this information is a blessing to you for years to come.

### First, you absolutely must use the right oil.

Maybe you've done some research on how best to season cast iron and discovered there really is no consensus about what oil or fat to use. You've read testimonies about how animal fat makes a seasoned surface that is too soft and to only ever use vegetable oils. Meanwhile, others say vegetable oils leave a sticky surface and to only use lard, or bacon grease – either of which I could never use because pig fat is not consistent with a Levitical dietary lifestyle.

Maybe family members have told you to never use butter while others claim butter works just fine. Some swear by Pam but others claim the additives in Pam leave a residue at high temperatures and pure canola oil is best. I've read that corn oil is the only thing to use, or grapeseed, or peanut, or extra virgin olive oil. Many recommend use of a saturated fat – that is, a fat that is solid at room temperature, whether it's animal or vegetable (palm oil, coconut oil, Crisco, lard).

Mostly, you'll read that it really doesn't matter what oil you use as long as you season your cast iron or purchase "pre-seasoned" cast iron.

What can I say? All of that is just plain wrong.

The truth is it really does matter what oil you use and the oil that gives the best results is none of the above. The absolute best oil to use is a food-grade flaxseed oil, preferably an organic cold pressed flaxseed oil.

The reason has to do with simple science. Artists and woodturners use linseed oil to protect wood or oil based paintings. Like flaxseed oil, linseed oil is a "drying oil," which means it can transform into a hard, tough film. In fact, it hardens to an impenetrable shell that keeps wood from getting nicked or turns oil paintings into solid images that can last for centuries. The problem is that linseed oil is not really safe to eat so you can't use it to season cast iron.

The food-grade equivalent of linseed oil is flaxseed oil. Flaxseed oil is ideal for seasoning cast iron for the same reason drying oils make an ideal base for oil paint and wood finishes. The scientific transformation from flaxseed oil to perfectly seasoned cast iron cookware is called "polymerization".

That wonderful nonstick "seasoning" on the surface of cast iron is formed by fat polymerization. Fat polymerization is maximized with a "drying oil" and flaxseed oil is the only drying oil on earth that's edible.

Be prepared to pay a premium for the flaxseed oil. It isn't cheap. At the time of this writing, an 18 ounce bottle of cold-pressed, unrefined, organic flaxseed oil from a healthfood store will cost about a dollar an ounce. Find it in the refrigerated section. Flaxseed oil goes rancid very quickly. Check the expiration date to ensure it hasn't already gone rancid. Store it in your refrigerator at home to keep it fresh. Right before you use it, shake it up very well just like the label says.

### Secondly, strip for success

If your cast iron is rusty or pitted, you should definitely strip it down to bare metal. If it is damaged or if it is left in a wet place, you may want to strip it before reseasoning it. If you picked up some cast iron in a second hand store or at a yard sale and it has a gummy or sticky thick coat or grease on it, you really should strip it and season it. Lastly, if you have never seasoned your cast iron with flaxseed oil, I would strongly recommend stripping it down, too. You will be amazed at the smooth, shiny, onyx black nonstick coating you will create in a relatively short time.

There are a lot of different methods to strip your cast iron. With all of them, the goal is to strip the cast iron enough to take it to the "vinegar step" which is the last step in stripping your cast iron before actually seasoning your metal. In all of the examples below, when I refer to steel wool I am referring to #0000 steel wool although some prefer nonmetallic scrub pads instead and that's fine, too.

So first, inspect your cast iron. Is it severely pitted and caked with years of gunk? Is it mildly rusted? Is it sticky with an uneven seasoning coat? Depending upon the condition, you may have to take serious steps to strip it down. Even the most coated caked on gunk is salvageable.

The ideal way to strip cast iron is through electrolysis, which cleans off both gunk and rust and leaves perfectly uniform gray iron metal behind. An electrolysis setup involves lots of electricity, a large plastic tub, stainless steel pipes, nonconductive shoes with grounding straps, and good ventilation. In other words, most of us do not have the luxury of electrolysis. However, if there are machine shops in your town or city, they may. Call or e-mail them and ask. It may be worth your time and trouble to arrange for them to affordably clean your cast iron using electrolysis.

The next best method is a lye bath, which cleans off gunk and old seasoning, but does not remove rust. Rust removal requires a second step. If you are comfortable with lye, this may be an option for you and it really does work. For me, this is not an option due to my sensible fear of industrial grade substances like lye that could explode and injure or kill me, my children, and pets.

If you're like me, and neither of the above are an option, for severely gunked cast iron you still may want to take drastic measures. For me, drastic means spray-on oven cleaner. If you opt for this method I urge you to use caution. This also may not be a good method to choose if you have small children or pets. Personally, this is the method of last resort because I hate using industrial grade chemicals of any kind but I must admit it can work to save your cast iron so I am including this method here. Basically, spray-on oven cleaner contains "safe" amounts of lye. That means that spray-on oven cleaner is one almost certain way to strip off decades of gunk and pitting.

Here's the idea. Take your badly damaged cast iron outside. Place it inside a plastic bag. Now suit up like an nuclear power plant worker with long rubber gloves (double, with thin latex underneath, in case there is a tear in the thick outer gloves), double mask over nose and mouth (one isn't enough – you will still breath vapors), and goggles over your eyes. Note that this is not excessive precaution or paranoia. Oven cleaner can burn right through your skin. It's lye with a liquid activator. It might be a good idea to have some vinegar or yogurt (which are both base or alkaline) handy to apply to your skin if it makes contact. Either of these can generally neutralize the acid in the oven cleaner.

Okay – using caution – and keeping from inhaling any fumes – apply a generous coating of spray-on oven cleaner to every surface of the cast iron inside the bag. Now seal the bag. About every other day for up to two weeks, suit up and reapply a generous portion of spray-on oven cleaner and reseal the bag. Be patient. Let the industrial grade toxic "safe" amounts of acids do the work for you.

After two weeks or less, wearing thick gloves and other safety gear, remove the pan so you can thoroughly rinse it off. NOTE: It will probably look like the rustiest piece of metal you can imagine but all the gunk should be long gone. Rinse it thoroughly and completely. Use some steel wool while rinsing to get rid of any remaining stubborn gunk and surface rust that the vinegar step will remove completely. Your cast iron should now be in a good state to take to the vinegar step.

Another method requires a self cleaning oven. This is a good method but there are some risks here, too. There have been reports of gunk from the cast iron catching fire inside the oven, which is locked during the cleaning cycle so you can't open it to put out the fire. There is also a risk of warping the cast iron if it is not well made. Self-cleaning temperatures are between 900-950° degrees F(480-510° degrees C). Most of the time, neither of these bad things happen and it works great but just be aware. You can plan ahead to minimize the risks. If your cast iron has decades of grease and gunk on it, this method will definitely create a lot of smoke, even if there is no fire, so you may want to take steel wool or use the salt and tater method described below to remove at least some of the grease beforehand.

To use the self cleaning oven method to strip your cast iron, you simply place the pan in the center of the oven upside down and set your oven to self-cleaning mode. Two hours later, or however long your self cleaning cycle runs, you should be ready to apply steel wool while rinsing or use the salt and tater method to get a uniform gray pan ready to take to the vinegar step.

If your cast iron is just a little rusty or maybe has an uneven seasoning coat, you can use the salt and tater method to strip it down. You'll need a coarse salt like kosher or sea salt, a few potatoes, and some flaxseed oil.

I personally also recommend gloves though they are optional.

Place your rusty skillet in the sink and sprinkle a couple tablespoons of coarse salt into it. Take your chunk of potato and start scrubbing right on top of the salt using the potato like a scrubbing pad or sponge.

The moisture from the potato will help the salt dig into the rust. The salt will get dirty very quickly. You may want to rinse out the pan after a bit just to survey your progress.

If there's still rust, pat everything dry, add more salt, and repeat the above step. Continue to the sides, edges, bottom and handle of your pan. Rinse thoroughly and pat dry.

When your cast iron is a uniform gray in color, the pan is ready to take to the vinegar step.

The vinegar step is very simple. You will need a container that can hold two gallons of water and the piece of cast iron you are preparing to season. I use my kitchen sink. You will need steel wool and you will need one quart of distilled white vinegar. You will need Washing Soda (NOT Baking Soda) to neutralize the vinegar.

The first step is to use hot soapy water and wash the cast iron like no one's business. Really enjoy this because you will likely never wash your cast iron with hot soapy water again unless you strip it all the way down again. Rinse it and pat it dry.

Now combine one quart of white vinegar in two gallons of clean water and soak your cast iron in this mixture for at least 30 minutes and up to 24 hours. What this will do is remove even microscopic rust from the piece. When you put a cast iron pan in a vinegar and water solution, it sort of simultaneously rusts and de-rusts. The vinegar will cause the excess rust to lift off the pan and bubble up, but when you take it out of the solution it instantly starts rusting because the iron is utterly unprotected and now exposed to oxygen. A very thin film of rust is unavoidable – you just oil the pan and wipe it off that way. Don't leave the pan in the vinegar indefinitely waiting for it to come out perfectly gray. It never will.

You want to leave the pan in the vinegar for the shortest time possible, so check it frequently, and never leave it in the vinegar solution for more than 24 hours. I checked the pan every couple of hours. With my worst skillet, at about the 12 hour mark I dumped out the rusty solution and put in new, clean solution. A few hours later, no more rust was bubbling up from the pan so I knew it was done.

After it's done soaking, remove it from the vinegar solution and lightly scrub every surface with steel wool or a nonmetallic scrubbing pad and washing soda to make sure the vinegar is completely neutralized. Washing soda is base; vinegar is acid. Also, whether you use steel wool or a scrub pad, the point is to just remove the surface rust the vinegar softened and brought to the surface in addition to neutralizing the vinegar. You are not trying to buff or polish the skillet to make it shiny. Seasoning will take care of that.

At this point the cast iron is perfectly ready to be seasoned. If you live in a humid environment you will need to begin the seasoning process just as soon as you have removed the rust. Untreated cast iron begins to rust immediately in damp climates. So, whichever method you used, the last step is to put your cast iron in a 200 degree oven to make sure it is bone dry. Remove it to a cooling rack and give it a light coat of flaxseed oil all over with a paper towel.

I want to emphasize how important it is at this point to get all the vinegar off and use washing soda to neutralize, thoroughly dry the pan, and then thoroughly oil it. Do not wait even 10 minutes to do this because the pan is already rusting and you must stop the process.

Rub the pan really well all over with oil – especially in any crevices – to wipe away the surface rust. Change paper towels frequently! You're cleaning the metal with the oil. When you stop seeing rust on the paper towel, you can start seasoning. Note that you'll still see dark residue from the iron before the pan is seasoned – that's normal.

Notice how the pan is a medium gray, and not the black usually associated with cast iron? That's because you've cleaned it down to the bare metal, which is gray. It's the seasoning that makes it dark. That comes next.

## Finally, seasoning is very different than cooking

Finally, time to season the skillet! But the things most really good cooks know as just common sense facts in the kitchen need to be set aside when seasoning. For one thing, good cooks know that heating any oil past it's smoke point causes a release of carcinogenic "free radicals" and for this reason most good cooks never get good results when attempting to season cast iron. The problem is that seasoning isn't cooking.

Good cooks are careful not to overheat polyunsaturated oil – and especially not any oils high in omega-3 fatty acids – because these oils are especially vulnerable to breakdown with heat and the release of free radicals. But it is exactly those oils, and that black smoke and carbon, and those free radicals in particular, especially alpha-linolenic acid (ALA) that enables polymerization. Drying oils, which produce the hardest polymers, are characterized by high levels of polyunsaturated fatty acids, especially the omega-3 fatty acid ALA. Flaxseed oil is 57% ALA. The cast iron seasoning process is an example of "radical polymerization". The process is initiated when heat energy is applied to iron in the presence of oxygen causing the release of free radicals in the oil. The free radicals then "crosslink" to form the tough, hard film you seek in a well-seasoned cast iron pan.

Free radicals are carcinogenic inside the human body. So don't ever heat oil you're going to eat above its smoke point. Ever. If the oil in the dish you are cooking even starts to smoke, toss it out and start over. But when you're seasoning cast iron, you're not cooking food, and you are not going to eat this oil. By the time a perfectly seasoned pan comes out of the oven, there should be no more free radicals.

## What to do for best results (and how to repair suboptimal results)

You will need a cooling rack, lots of paper towels, your oven, oven mitts, and cold-pressed organic flaxseed oil. Place your cast iron in the center of your cold oven and heat it to 220° degrees F (105° degrees C). You heat the pan in the oven to be sure it's bone dry and to open the pores of the iron a little.

Then put it on a paper towel on top of a cooling rack, pour a little flaxseed oil on it (don't forget to shake the bottle), and rub the oil all over the pan making sure to get into every nook and cranny. Your hands and the pan will be nice and oily.

Now rub it all off.

You read that right. All. Off. Rub it off with paper towels or a cotton cloth until it looks like there is nothing left on the surface. There actually is still oil left on the surface, it's just very thin. The pan should look dry, not glistening with oil. Put the pan upside down in a cold oven. Most instructions say to put aluminum foil under it to catch any drips, but if your oil coating is as thin as it should be, there won't be any drips.

Turn the oven to a baking temperature of as high as your oven goes up to 500° degrees F (260° degrees C) and let the pan preheat with the oven. The reason for the very hot oven is to be sure the temperature is above the oil's smoke point, and to profoundly accelerate the release of free radicals. Unrefined flaxseed oil actually has the lowest smoke point of any oil. But the higher the temperature the more it will smoke, and that's good for seasoning.

When it reaches temperature, set the timer for an hour. After an hour, turn off the oven but don't open the oven door. Let it cool off with the pan inside for two hours, at which point it's cool enough to handle.

The pan will come out of the oven a little darker, but matte in texture – not the semigloss you're aiming for. It needs more coats. In fact, it needs at least six coats. So again rub on the oil, wipe it off, put it in the cold oven, let it preheat, bake for an hour, and let it cool in the oven for two hours. At that point it starts to develop a bit of a sheen and the pan is ready for use.

If you try this, you may be tempted to use a thicker coat of oil to speed up the process. Don't do it. It just results in an uneven surface – or worse, baked on drips. Bottom line: you can't speed up the process. If you try, you'll mess up the pan and have to start over.

I mentioned earlier there's a myth floating around that vegetable oils leave a sticky residue. If the pan comes out of the oven sticky, the cause is one of three things:

1. You put the oil on too thick.

2. Your oven temperature was too low.

3. Your baking time was too short.

It's possible to use a suboptimal oil for seasoning, like Crisco® or butter, and still end up with a usable pan. Many (most) people do this. But the seasoning will be relatively soft, not as nonstick, and will tend to wear off. If you want the hardest, slickest seasoning possible, use the right oil: flaxseed oil.

When you're finished, the seasoned coating is smooth, hard, and evenly colored.

# Fish!

Growing up in a family from the Pacific Northwest, fresh fish is one of my favorite proteins. I especially love Rainbow Trout and Salmon.

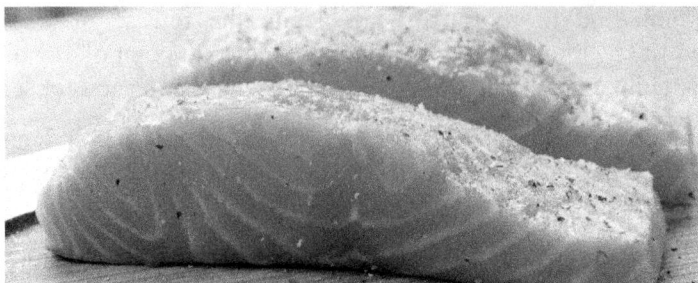

When buying fish, there are two options: wild caught or farm raised.

*Farm Raised Fish:* Farmers raise fish commercially in tanks and/or enclosures in lakes, ponds, rivers and oceans. Due to the cramped space being taken up by so many fish, they tend to have more diseases and toxins. To combat the diseases and toxins, they're given antibiotics. And, because they can't move around like wild caught fish, they contain more fat.

*Wild caught fish* tend to be higher in Omega 3 fatty acids, protein and contain very low levels of disease. Because they're not controlled, they have no antibiotics, pesticides, or artificial dyes. Wild caught also have less fat than farm raised fish.

While you may pay more for wild caught fish, you're getting a much better, safer, and cleaner product for your dollar.

When you buy whole fish, make sure the eyes are not sunken or cloudy. Don't be afraid to touch and inspect the fish. It should have a firm body that is springy to the touch and only a mild smell. A "fishy" smell is something to be avoided.

If you're buying fish that is already cut into fillets or steaks, it should have firm, elastic and moist-looking flesh. The skin should be shiny and bright. Again, it should only have a mild smell - nothing "fishy".

When you purchase fish, you should prepare it within one or two days. It is highly perishable.

# BATTERED COD

My kids all love fried fish. The trick to this recipe is to use fresh, not frozen, cod. If you use frozen, you're likely to end up with a soggy mess. Fresh fish will cook perfectly inside the shell of crispy fried dough.

### INGREDIENTS:

2 $\frac{1}{2}$ pounds cod fillets, cut into individual portions

1 $\frac{1}{2}$ cup flour (I use fresh ground soft white wheat)

1 $\frac{1}{2}$ tsp aluminum-free baking powder

2 tsp sugar or honey (pure, raw, local honey is always best)

2 tsp salt (Kosher or sea salt is best)

1 cup filtered water

1 farm fresh egg

Organic grapeseed oil, peanut oil, or rice oil for frying

### SUPPLIES:

| | |
|---|---|
| large skillet | measuring cups/spoons |
| bowl | slotted spoon |
| whisk | paper towel lined plate |

### PREPARATION:

Cut the fish into individual portions.

Heat 1 inch of oil in a large deep iron skillet over medium heat until hot but not smoking.

### DIRECTIONS:

In a large bowl, combine flour, baking powder, honey (or sugar), salt, water, and egg. Mix well with whisk.

Dip the cod fillets into the batter, coating completely, then fry in the oil for 4 to 5 minutes per side, or until the coating is golden and the fish flakes easily with a fork.

Drain on a paper towel-lined platter. Serve immediately.

### YIELD:

Serves: 4

NUTRITION:

| Nutrition Facts | |
|---|---|
| Serving Size 376 g | |
| **Amount Per Serving** | |
| Calories 436 | Calories from Fat 59 |
| | % Daily Value* |
| Total Fat 6.6g | 10% |
| Saturated Fat 0.8g | 4% |
| *Trans* Fat 0.0g | |
| Cholesterol 154mg | 51% |
| Sodium 1547mg | 64% |
| Total Carbohydrates 35.8g | 12% |
| Dietary Fiber 5.5g | 22% |
| Sugars 3.1g | |
| Protein 57.9g | |
| Vitamin A 2% • | Vitamin C 0% |
| Calcium 14% • | Iron 11% |
| Nutrition Grade B | |
| * Based on a 2000 calorie diet | |

Low in saturated fat

Low in sugar

High in manganese

NOTES:

This recipe specifically calls for cod; however, any white fish will do.

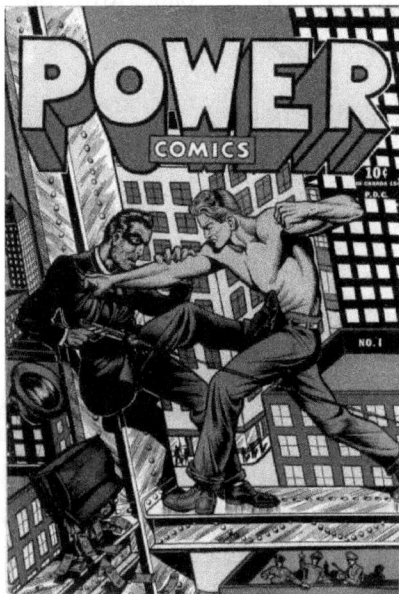

## CAPTAIN TOOTSIE TUNA & CORN SKILLET

# TUNA & CORN SKILLET

This recipe produces a sauce that you serve over rice. The tuna and corn combine together to create a wonderful flavor combination. It is a quick meal that is perfect for one of those busy week day nights.

INGREDIENTS:

12 $^1/_4$ oz (1 can) tuna in water, drained and flaked

2 $^1/_2$ TBS unsalted butter

1 small onion

$^1/_2$ cup milk

12 ounces frozen organic corn

1 $^1/_2$ cup Hallee's Homemade Cream of Mushroom Soup ⓘ

$^1/_4$ tsp freshly ground black pepper

SUPPLIES:

large skillet                          measuring cups/spoons
sharp knife/cutting board              wooden spoon

PREPARATION:

Chop onion ⓘ

Prepare cream of mushroom soup

DIRECTIONS:

In a large skillet, melt butter over medium heat. Add onion and saute 2 to 3 minutes, until tender and translucent.

Stir in soup and milk. Add corn, tuna, and pepper; heat through, stirring occasionally.

Serve over hot cooked rice.

YIELD:

Makes about 4 cups. (Serves: 4)

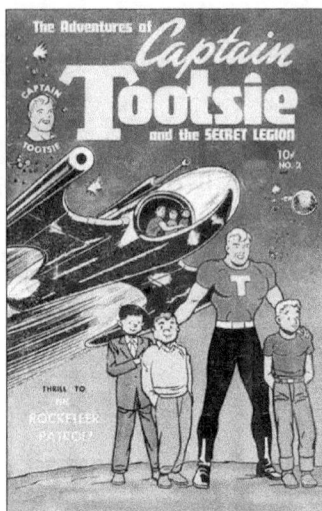

NUTRITION:

## Nutrition Facts

Serving Size 320 g

Amount Per Serving

| Calories 315 | Calories from Fat 129 |
|---|---|
| | % Daily Value* |
| Total Fat 13.9g | 21% |
| Saturated Fat 6.4g | 32% |
| Cholesterol 59mg | 20% |
| Sodium 407mg | 17% |
| Total Carbohydrates 24.1g | 8% |
| Dietary Fiber 2.3g | 9% |
| Sugars 7.8g | |
| Protein 25.3g | |

| Vitamin A 6% | • | Vitamin C 14% |
|---|---|---|
| Calcium 6% | • | Iron 8% |

Very high in selenium

Very high in vitamin B6

NOTES:

① I have also included a recipe for Hallee's Homemade Cream of Mushroom Soup in this cookbook. If you don't have it on hand and have no time to whip up a batch, be sure to use a good organic soup with low or no salt. If you would like to make your own batch, follow this link:

http://www.halleethehomemaker.com/cream-of-mushroom

# HOT TUNA STEAKS ❋ ⏱ ✝ 🫛 ✡ 🍬 🚫 🌍 🍷 🍲 🍽

Tuna steaks make a perfect "company's coming" meal. The meat is so rich and packed with all sorts of good-for-you Omega 3's and protein. The kick of the peppercorns and the accompaniment of the orange garlic mayonnaise is the perfect flavor combination.

### INGREDIENTS:

6 tuna steaks (6 to 8 ounces each), cut 1 inch thick

2 TBS extra virgin olive oil

2 TBS fresh lemon juice

$1/4$ cup whole black peppercorns

freshly ground black pepper, to taste

salt (Kosher or sea salt is best), to taste

Roasted Orange Garlic Mayonnaise ⓘ (optional), for serving

### SUPPLIES:

Chef knife and cutting board -OR-mortar and pedestal

Large bowl

Measuring cups/spoons

Large plate

Large skillet

### PREPARATION:

Using the mortar and pedestal, or the flat of the chef knife, crush the pepper. The peppercorns should be crushed, not ground.

### DIRECTIONS:

Place the tuna in a bowl to fit. Add the oil, lemon juice, salt and pepper. Turn the tuna to coat well in the marinade. Let rest 15 to 20 minutes, turning once.

Place peppercorns on a large plate.

When ready to cook the tuna, dip the edges into the crushed peppercorns.

Heat skillet over medium heat. Brush the bottom of the skillet with olive oil.

Add 2 to 3 Tablespoons of marinade to the skillet. Sear the tuna steaks, in batches if necessary, for 4 minutes per side for medium-rare fish.

Serve dolloped with Roasted Orange Garlic Mayonnaise (optional).

YIELD:

Serves 6

NUTRITION:

## Nutrition Facts

Serving Size 182 g

**Amount Per Serving**

| Calories 358 | Calories from Fat 139 |
|---|---|
| | % Daily Value* |
| Total Fat 15.4g | 24% |
| Saturated Fat 3.5g | 17% |
| Cholesterol 83mg | 28% |
| Sodium 87mg | 4% |
| Total Carbohydrates 1.2g | 0% |
| Protein 51.1g | |

| Vitamin A 86% | • | Vitamin C 4% |
|---|---|---|
| Calcium 2% | • | Iron 15% |

Nutrition Grade A-

* Based on a 2000 calorie diet

Low in sodium
Very low in sugar
Very high in niacin
High in phosphorus
Very high in selenium
Very high in vitamin A
High in vitamin B6
Very high in vitamin B12

NOTES:

Coat only the edges of the tuna steaks before cooking. Be careful not to overcook the fish or it will dry out.

LONG JOHN SILVER TILAPIA WITH TOMATO OLIVE SAUCE
## TILAPIA WITH TOMATO OLIVE SAUCE

These tilapia fillets are perfect topped with a savory tomato-olive sauce that comes together in just 5 minutes. Look for tapenade near jarred olives in the supermarket.

**INGREDIENTS:**

1 $\frac{1}{4}$ lbs tilapia

$\frac{1}{4}$ cup dry white wine ⓘ (see NOTES for substitute)

1 pint ripe grape or cherry tomatoes

3 cloves garlic

2 TBS extra virgin olive oil, divided

3 TBS kalamata olive tapenade

$\frac{1}{4}$ tsp freshly ground black pepper

$\frac{1}{4}$ tsp salt (Kosher or sea salt is best)

**SUPPLIES:**

Large skillet

Sharp knife/cutting board

Measuring cups/spoons

Serving platter/foil

**PREPARATION:**

Slice tomatoes in half

Chop garlic

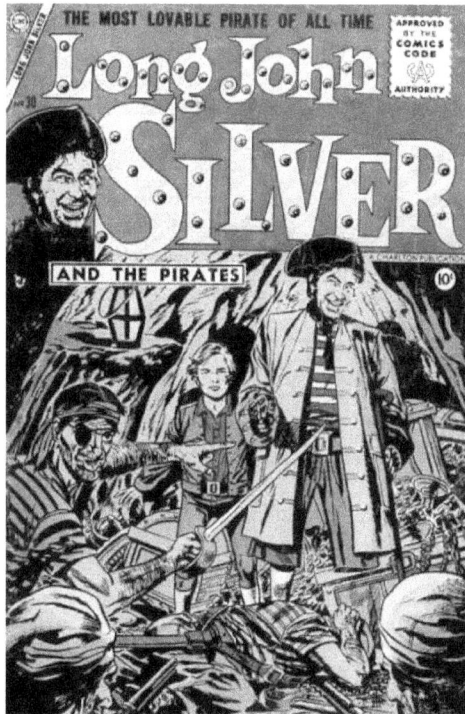

## DIRECTIONS:

Sprinkle tilapia with salt and pepper.

Heat 1 tablespoon oil in a large skillet over medium-high heat. Add the fish and cook (in two batches if necessary), turning once halfway through, until golden brown and just opaque in the center, 4 to 6 minutes total.

Transfer the fish to a serving platter; tent with foil to keep warm.

Off the heat, add the remaining 1 tablespoon oil, tomatoes, wine, and garlic to the pan.

Return to medium heat, cover, and cook, stirring occasionally, until most of tomatoes are broken down, 4 to 5 minutes.

Stir in olive tapenade and cook for 1 minute more.

Serve the fish with the sauce.

## YIELD:

Individual yield can be weight or item, depending on the size.

## NUTRITION:

| Nutrition Facts | |
|---|---|
| Serving Size 253 g | |

| Amount Per Serving | |
|---|---|
| Calories 271 | Calories from Fat 135 |
| | % Daily Value* |
| Total Fat 15.0g | 23% |
| Saturated Fat 2.5g | 13% |
| Trans Fat 0.0g | |
| Cholesterol 69mg | 23% |
| Sodium 507mg | 21% |
| Total Carbohydrates 4.6g | 2% |
| Dietary Fiber 1.4g | 6% |
| Sugars 1.1g | |
| Protein 27.5g | |
| Vitamin A 10% | Vitamin C 26% |
| Calcium 3% | Iron 11% |

Low in sugar

High in Vitamin C

## NOTES:

ⓘ If you abstain from alcohol even in cooking, you can substitute a 100% pure grape juice (ensure there is no apple juice in it) and one tsp of distilled vinegar to approximate the same flavor and properties while cooking.

## FIVE-SPICE TILAPIA

⏱ ✡ 🜂 ❋ 🌐 📷

Chinese five-spice powder, soy sauce, and brown sugar make a quick, spicy-sweet glaze for tilapia. Serve with rice for a wonderful quick meal.

INGREDIENTS:

1 lb tilapia fillets

1 tsp Chinese five-spice powder ⓘ (See NOTES)

$^1/_4$ cup soy sauce (Tamari or fermented soy sauce strongly preferred)

3 TBS light brown sugar or honey (pure, raw, local honey is always best)

1 TBS organic grapeseed oil, peanut oil, or rice oil

3 scallions

SUPPLIES:

Sharp knife/cutting board

Measuring cups/spoons

Small bowl/whisk

Large skillet

PREPARATION:

Slice scallions in thin slices

DIRECTIONS:

Sprinkle both sides of tilapia fillets with five-spice powder. Combine soy sauce and brown sugar in a small bowl with whisk.

Heat oil in a large skillet over medium-high heat. Add the tilapia and cook until the outer edges are opaque, about 2 minutes.

Reduce heat to medium, turn the fish over, stir the soy mixture, and pour into the pan. Bring the sauce to a boil and cook until the fish is cooked through and the sauce has thickened slightly, about 2 minutes more. Add scallions and remove from the heat.

Serve the fish drizzled with the pan sauce.

**CAPTAIN VIDEO**

"THE TIME WHEN MEN COULD NOT WALK!"

**YIELD:**

Serves 4

**NUTRITION:**

## Nutrition Facts

Serving Size 182 g

| Amount Per Serving | |
|---|---|
| Calories 183 | Calories from Fat 41 |
| | % Daily Value* |
| Total Fat 4.5g | 7% |
| Saturated Fat 0.9g | 5% |
| Trans Fat 0.0g | |
| Cholesterol 55mg | 18% |
| Sodium 1026mg | 43% |
| Total Carbohydrates 15.0g | 5% |
| Sugars 13.5g | |
| Protein 22.4g | |
| Vitamin A 2% • | Vitamin C 4% |
| Calcium 3% • | Iron 9% |

High in selenium

**NOTES:**

ⓘ Five-spice powder is a blend of cloves, cinnamon, star anise, fennel seed, and Szechuan peppercorns. Look for it in the spice section at the market or with other Asian ingredients.

Making your own is quite easy. Try using the recipe in the back of this cookbook.

# TIGHT TIMES TUNA CASSEROLE

This is THE EASIEST meal you can make for your family. My children love it. They get seconds and thirds. Throw it on a plate with some green peas and a garden salad, and you have a healthy, home cooked meal that takes you as long as it takes the macaroni to boil.

INGREDIENTS:

1 pound whole grain elbow macaroni

1 can tuna in oil

2 cups Can-Do "No Cans" Cream of Mushroom Soup ⓘ or 1 can cream of mushroom soup

$^1/_4$ cup diced onion

$^1/_4$ cup diced green pepper

2 TBS extra virgin olive oil

2 tsp Kosher or sea salt

SUPPLIES:

deep skillet

large saucepan

colander

wooden spoon

sharp knife and cutting board

PREPARATION:

dice onion and green pepper [link to dicer]

DIRECTIONS:

Cook macaroni according to package directions. Put about 1 TBS olive oil and 2 tsp salt in the water before adding the macaroni.

While the macaroni is cooking, heat 1 TBS olive oil in the frying pan over medium to medium-high heat. Add the onion and green pepper.

Cook, stirring, until the onion is clear and soft. Add the tuna (do not drain).

Stir in the soup. Add the cooked macaroni. Stir until combined.

 YIELD:

Serves 6

 NUTRITION:

| Nutrition Facts | |
| --- | --- |
| Serving Size 109 g | |
| **Amount Per Serving** | |
| **Calories** 210 | Calories from Fat 49 |
| | **% Daily Value**\* |
| **Total Fat** 5.4g | **8%** |
| Saturated Fat 1.0g | **5%** |
| *Trans* Fat 0.0g | |
| **Cholesterol** 5mg | **2%** |
| **Sodium** 479mg | **20%** |
| **Total Carbohydrates** 30.2g | **10%** |
| Dietary Fiber 1.3g | **5%** |
| Sugars 1.5g | |
| **Protein** 9.3g | |
| Vitamin A 1%  •  Vitamin C 3% | |
| Calcium 1%  •  Iron 9% | |
| **Nutrition Grade B** | |
| \* Based on a 2000 calorie diet | |

Very high in selenium
High in niacin
High in thiamin
Low in sugar
Very low in cholesterol

 NOTES:

You can use any kind of pasta — medium shells are nice – they capture the sauce nicely. I've used tri-colored rotini. Any small, bite-sized pasta.

ⓘ For your convenience, I have included the recipe for Can-Do "No Cans" Cream of Mushroom Soup in the back of this cookbook. Try it. You may never buy a can of soup again.

> TIP: Store your cast iron in the oven to prevent rusting. It works better in gas stoves with pilot lights that keep the moisture out of the air.

## CORNMEAL CRUSTED RAINBOW TROUT

My dad tells the story of his early marriage to my mom, when he went fishing in the McKenzie River in the Willamette Valley in Oregon and came home with a mess of rainbow trout that he just dumped into the kitchen sink. Her response to that was, "What do you expect me to do with that?" To which he often follows up with, "You're lucky you made it here, Hallee. There was a moment there that you might never have been."

My mom never has enjoyed rainbow trout, but (after my dad would clean fish well away from mom's kitchen sink) she would fry it in cornmeal. When I bit into this dish, I was immediately transported back in time to my childhood and eating fresh caught rainbow trout.

INGREDIENTS:

4 rainbow trout fillets, skin on

cornmeal

salt and pepper

extra virgin olive oil

1 lemon

SUPPLIES:

skillet                    plate
lemon juicer               paper towels

## PREPARATION:

Salt and pepper the fish. Sprinkle with cornmeal and press down.

## DIRECTIONS:

Heat about a tablespoon of olive oil in your pan. Heat it just under medium-high heat. Add the fish, skin side up.

Cook for 4 minutes. Flip over and cook for 2 minutes.

Remove from the heat and place on paper towels. Repeat with the remaining 2 fillets, adding a little more oil if needed.

Drizzle with fresh squeezed lemon.

## YIELD:

Serves 4

## NUTRITION:

| Nutrition Facts | |
|---|---|
| Serving Size 115 g | |

| Amount Per Serving | |
|---|---|
| **Calories** 222 | Calories from Fat 124 |
| | **% Daily Value\*** |
| **Total Fat** 13.8g | **21%** |
| Saturated Fat 2.9g | **15%** |
| *Trans* Fat 0.1g | |
| **Cholesterol** 64mg | **21%** |
| **Sodium** 49mg | **2%** |
| **Total Carbohydrates** 1.3g | **0%** |
| **Protein** 24.1g | |
| Vitamin A 2%  •  Vitamin C 2% | |
| Calcium 2%  •  Iron 2% | |
| \* Based on a 2000 calorie diet | |

Low in sodium
Very low in sugar
High in thiamin
Very low in cholesterol

## NOTES:

I have also used grapeseed oil to fry these fish in – or a mixture of both extra virgin olive oil and grapeseed oil.

## BEEF AND LAMB AND GAME OH MY

# Red Meat!

One great thing about cooking with cast iron is how it allows you to get a really great sear on the outside of your meat. That sear locks in all the juices and flavor and allows the steak to cook perfectly. In fact, other than perhaps stainless steel, it is one of the only ways to get that great outside sear while indoors in the kitchen other than specialty items like a rotisserie oven. Actually, when I rotisserie a roast, I still sear the outside first and it is even more delicious!

Here are some quick "Do's and Dont's" when it comes to cooking absolutely amazing red meat using cast iron.

## KINDS, CUTS, & GRADES OF RED MEATS

Red meats commonly include cuts of beef just like you can purchase at your corner grocer as well as lamb and goat in specialty butcher shops. Red meat also includes traditional game meats such as bison and venison. There are different cuts and grades of red meat and some are going to cook better than others in certain recipes.

When it comes to red meat, the most important step in preparing, for example, the perfect steak is to first PURCHASE a really great steak. If you don't start with "top" red meat, you aren't going to end up with that amazing great flavor that will soon be your signature. Bottom line: be very, very choosy about your red meat purchase.

The "best" cuts come from the "top" of – or "high" on – the animal which is where we get the ironic expression "living high on the hog" for instance. Top sirloin, for instance, means that the cut came from the upper rear part of the animal as opposed to bottom sirloin, which is properly called the flank or suet cut. The top cuts are the best roasts and thickest most juicy and delicious steaks.

The "low cuts" come from "where the sun doesn't shine" on the animal. They may require some additional preparation to make them tender as a main course but work great in stir dishes like fajitas, strips over couscous, or in stews and chilis.

When buying high cuts such as ribeye, sirloin, prime, or rump, look for meat that has some fat marbling around the edges. Expect it to be pricey. Try to keep in mind that it is going to taste absolutely amazing. Even though it feels like a high price to pay for a meal, in the case of a perfect steak it will ultimately cost you less than a dinner out for 1 at any 5-star chop-house.

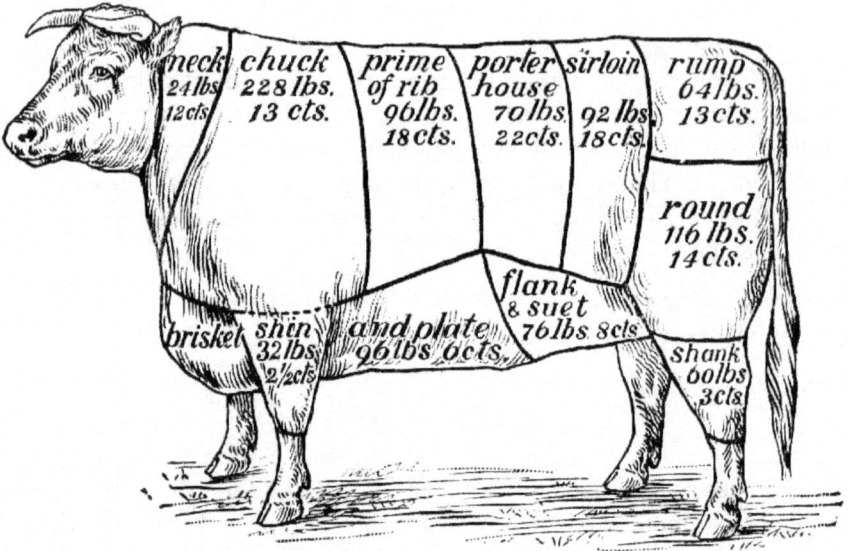

Keep in mind, too, that a single pound of steak can easily feed 2 and often stretch (cut thin and fanned with delicious sides) to feed 4 adults.

In the United States, cuts can be voluntarily graded by the Department of Agriculture according to USDA standards ⓘ. USDA meat grading is voluntary and the meat packing plants have to pay for grading so that cost is passed along to the consumers. The eight possible USDA grades for beef from best to worst are Prime, Choice, Select, Standard, Commercial, Utility, Cutter, and Canner while chicken, turkey, duck, and other inspected game birds like geese and pigeon can be graded with the letter system graded from A to F.

The vast majority of widely available graded beef in groceries across these United States is graded Standard. While Standard cuts are very good, when purchasing USDA graded beef, try to purchase at least Select and expect to pay more for Choice and far more for Prime cuts (which are usually reserved for 5-star restaurants). There is no significance to USDA Grade A beef anymore than USDA Choice chicken, so read labeling carefully to avoid clever marketing.

Often times, you can obtain very high quality meat equal to or better than

USDA graded cuts at a reduced cost when you purchase from a local butcher, preferably one who either raises the animals himself or sources cuts from local sustainable farms. The animal should be at least partially grass-fed and humanely butchered.

When it comes to Choice or Prime beef – especially steaks – if at all possible, purchase cuts that have been dry-aged to intensify the flavor. The best steaks are dry aged for at least a few weeks.

## TENDERIZERS

Commonly used kitchen tools such as tenderizing meat mallets and hammers and the recent use of the lacerating meat tenderizers that puncture the meat with dozens of sharp needles or blades for marinates have their place in cooking red meats. Their place is always for low cuts that you intend to marinate for a day or more. Never use any such tools on any of the high cuts. The result will be a very dry, tough, and overdone beef dish that could have otherwise been a delicious top dish.

On low cuts like plate, flank, skirt, shank, and even some round cuts, you might want to tenderize the meat with a mallet or hammer or use a lacerating meat tenderizer then place it in a marinade to baste for a day or two prior to cooking. A good marinade will further tenderize and deeply infuse an otherwise often plain cut of red meat with delightful and unique flavor.

I've included a simple and very effective alcohol free Red Meat Marinade recipe in this cookbook. Feel free to use that recipe when marinating your low cuts or expand on it by adding your own preferred seasonings and spices. Try using an inexpensive red or white wine to the recipe for a signature flavor of your own.

## PRECOOKING TEMPERATURE

Steam cooking red meat does not make a nicely browned crispy outside sear that locks in all that flavor or a perfect rare, medium-rare, or medium throughout cut of meat. Steam cooking red meat results in a gray kind of mushy outside layer and the inside does not cook evenly. Instead of a perfect medium or medium rare, it will turn out a bit tough or chewy with pockets of meat that range from rare to well done.

So, the idea is to never let your red meat steam cook. Fortunately, cast iron is perfectly ideal for this with just a little preparation on your part.

Before you cook your red meat, it must first reach room temperature throughout. It must not be even cold to the touch and definitely not frozen. Frozen meat will have ice crystals inside that will melt and then steam the meat while cooking, making it alternately tough and mushy.

If your steaks are frozen, put them in the refrigerator to defrost for at least a day or two in advance. This will allow the ice crystals inside the frozen meat to thaw and let you better remove any excess water before cooking.

Remember, the best steaks are actually dry aged for up to a few weeks. For us at home, though, no red meat should sit out above 42° degrees F (5.5° degrees C) and below 165° degrees F (75° degrees C) for more than four hours. So, within reason, the longer it sits out, the better. Remove meat from the refrigerator at least 30 minutes or longer depending on the cut and thickness, before you intend to cook it and allow it to assume room temperature.

Once the meat reaches room temperature, you need to get it completely dry. If necessary, drain any juices from the steak packaging. You can preserve these drippings if you are making an au jus or a gravy.

Blot your red meat perfectly dry with paper towels or a clean kitchen towel. Try to end up with meat thoroughly dried of any water or moisture before cooking. If your beef is at all damp, you will essentially be steam cooking it and you will not be pleased with the result.

## RUBS: SALT & WATER ARE NOT YOUR FRIENDS

Because you are cooking cuts of red meat and not, say, an entire chicken or turkey, the red meat cuts are often less fatty than, for example, cooking bone in chicken thighs. In that case you often have the advantage of cooking the bird in its own fatty skin. Consequently, it is often advisable to lightly coat your red meat with a fat such as unsalted butter or extra virgin olive oil.

Lamb and goat will have the most fat when cooked. Game meat such as bison and venison is very lean and will have less fat. So, you will want to very lightly coat a rack of lamb, for example, while you may want to whisk together melted butter and extra virgin olive oil and slather it on thick when preparing venison.

It is fine to cook red meat with just that light coating of oil or fat and no additional seasoning. It will taste great and cook up just fine. But it is likely that you will want to add a tasty dry rub over the coating to create a signature flavor that no one will ever forget. This is where you can really experiment with some incredibly tasty rubs.

I've included recipes for Montreal Steak Seasoning and Cajun-Creole

Seasoning in this cookbook which are written so that they can easily be mixed into marvelous red meat rubs. As you will see, the secret to making a great dry spice rub is never, ever to include salt. Try these or expand on them by adding your own preferred seasonings and spices.

You should not – as in never, ever – salt red meat BEFORE cooking it. Salt brings moisture (water) to the surface of the steak. That water sits on the surface as you cook the steak. Thus, you are once again basically steaming the meat which is the last thing you want to do. Outside on the grill, the meat always ends up too well done and a bit dry. Inside, it usually ends up mushy and gray. By leaving off the salt before cooking, the result will be juicy, delicious steaks and roasts.

Feel free to add a dash of Kosher or sea salt to taste after your meat or steak is cooked to your liking, has rested the required time, and add only just before serving.

I always recommend Kosher salt and it is always my first choice. First of all, it's white in color but Kosher salt also, in my opinion, is the lightest and most versatile salt. Real sea salt is rich in additional minerals which are very good for our health and depending on those minerals it will often look pink, brown, or gray in color. In my experience, sea salt will also work but is better suited to dishes like homemade chips and crackers or raw vegetables that may be lacking minerals than to meat dishes which are packed with nutrition. Iodized table salt contains iodine that often creates an undesirable color and flavor when reacting with other ingredients, particularly tomatoes.

There's only one thing you should **never** attempt using cast iron cookware: **boiling water** which will cause it to rust.

IRON SKILLET
MAN SAYS...

NOTES:

ⓘ For the latest information about the current Agricultural Marketing Service USDA standards for grading meat and other consumable commodities, visit the official website at:
http://www.ams.usda.gov/AMSv1.0/Grading

# Low Cuts!

Always purchase the best cut of meat you can afford. Sometimes, though, that sale on flank, rump, or shank is too good to pass up! Never fear. Low cuts are great for soups, stews, and chilis. Marinated red meats are the perfect choice for rice and pasta dishes.

Now that you have settled on a red meat dish, when performing your menu planning you will want to give some thought to what recipe you are going to serve. If you are using an inexpensive cut of meat, planning ahead allows you to season or marinate it for an unforgettably good flavor. There is no need for a boxed "helper" when you can inexpensively and quickly serve up whole, real food to your hungry family.

*round 116 lbs. 14 cts.*

*flank & suet 76 lbs. 8 cts.*

*brisket shin 32 lbs 2½ cts*

*and plate 96 lbs 6 cts.*

*shank 60 lbs 3 cts*

This section of recipes is dedicated to the go-to home cooked inexpensive meals that are just packed with flavor and nutrition. A perfectly seared, perfectly cooked medium-rare one inch thick prime top cut need not be the centerpiece of every meal. Besides, we'll get to those later.

TIP: Although everything from Dutch ovens to cactus-shaped cornbread pans comes in cast iron, nothing is more versatile than a basic skillet. Either a 10- or 12-inch will do.

## CAMP OUT DUTCH OVEN CHILI

Chili is great for parties or any kind of gatherings whether it's cool outside or not. You can always freeze leftovers in various sized bags to warm up for a quick meal, to top hot dogs, or even to top baked potatoes.

Coarsely chopping your own steak or grinding a roast into your own ground beef makes a heartier chili. You could substitute some or all of the beef for venison or bison for more amazing flavor.

### INGREDIENTS:

7 to 8 lbs round steak, cut into 1-inch pieces

(or about 6-7 lbs of lean ground beef)

4 cups beef broth or beef stock

$\frac{1}{4}$ cup extra virgin olive oil

$\frac{1}{4}$ cup unsalted butter

$\frac{1}{4}$ cup flour (I use fresh ground soft white wheat)

8 poblano peppers, roasted, peeled and chopped

4 cups diced onion, finely chopped ⓘ

4 large tomatoes, chopped

8 cloves garlic, crushed

1 TBS chopped fresh tarragon

2 TBS ground cumin

2 TBS paprika

1 TBS freshly ground black pepper

2 TBS salt (Kosher or sea salt is best)

### SUPPLIES:

8 quart Dutch Oven

measuring cups/spoons

good sharp knife

cutting board

baking sheet

**PREPARATION:**

Roast the poblano peppers:

Position rack in upper third of oven and preheat oven on broil, or bring to about 500° degrees F (260° degrees C). Place peppers on a baking sheet and roast under the broiler about 10 to 15 minutes until charred and softened, turning every 5 minutes. Place in brown paper bag and seal, letting the peppers cool. Transfer to a clean cutting board. Peel and chop peppers into bite-size pieces.

If you are grinding your meat into ground beef, go ahead and grind it now.

## DIRECTIONS:

In an 8 qt. camp Dutch oven over medium heat, add the olive oil. Add onions and cook until onions are soft. Dip onions out.

Dredge meat in flour, salt and pepper. Add the butter to Dutch oven and melt. Immediately place dredged meat in Dutch oven, stirring continuously until beef is browned.

Return cooked onions to pan; add garlic. Stir and brown 2 to 3 minutes. Add cumin, paprika, tarragon, pablano peppers, tomatoes, beef broth and enough water to cover completely. Bring to a boil.

Cover and simmer from 2 $\frac{1}{2}$ hours or until tender, stirring occasionally, adding a little water as needed.

## YIELD:

About 8 to 10 servings

## NUTRITION:

| Nutrition Facts | |
|---|---|
| Serving Size 105 g | |
| **Amount Per Serving** | |
| Calories 138 | Calories from Fat 44 |
| | % Daily Value* |
| Total Fat 4.9g | 8% |
| Saturated Fat 2.0g | 10% |
| Cholesterol 58mg | 19% |
| Sodium 341mg | 14% |
| Total Carbohydrates 2.5g | 1% |
| Dietary Fiber 0.5g | 2% |
| Sugars 0.9g | |
| Protein 19.8g | |
| Vitamin A 5% • | Vitamin C 30% |
| Calcium 1% • | Iron 68% |
| * Based on a 2000 calorie diet | |

Low in sugar

Very high in iron

High in niacin

High in phosphorus

Very high in selenium

Very high in vitamin B6

Very high in vitamin B12

Very high in vitamin C

High in zinc

## NOTES:

ⓘ For information about a tip for chopping vegetables, follow this link:
http://www.halleethehomemaker.com/chopping-veg

## POTATO PEPPER STEAK           ❄ ⏱ ✡ 🌾 🍽

It's always nice to find a recipe that makes an easy, filling meal. This dish is just that. Serve it with some warmed French Bread and a salad and you have an entire meal.

**INGREDIENTS:**

1 lb beef chuck steak

4 medium-sized potatoes, peeled and thinly sliced

1 large green bell pepper

2 garlic cloves

3 TBS extra virgin olive oil, divided

2 TBS soy sauce (Tamari or fermented soy sauce strongly preferred)

$1/2$ tsp salt (Kosher or sea salt is best)

$1/4$ tsp fresh ground black pepper

**SUPPLIES:**

Sharp knife/cutting board

Large skillet

**PREPARATION:**

Thinly slice the steak.

Peel and slice the potatoes

Cut the pepper into $1/4$ inch strips

Mince the garlic

**DIRECTIONS:**

In a large skillet, heat 2 tablespoons oil over medium-high heat. Add potatoes and sprinkle with salt and pepper. Sauté for 12 to 15 minutes, or until golden, turning halfway through cooking.

Remove to a platter and cover to keep warm.

Add remaining 1 tablespoon oil to skillet then add the steak, garlic, and bell pepper. Increase the heat to high and sauté for 4 to 5 minutes, or until steak is cooked to desired doneness. Add soy sauce, and stir to coat. Cook for 1 minute then spoon steak and pepper mixture over potatoes.

NUTRITION:

# Nutrition Facts

Serving Size 389 g

| Amount Per Serving | |
|---|---|
| Calories 417 | Calories from Fat 170 |
| | % Daily Value* |
| Total Fat 18.9g | 29% |
| Saturated Fat 4.0g | 20% |
| Cholesterol 70mg | 23% |
| Sodium 832mg | 35% |
| Potassium 979mg | 28% |
| Total Carbohydrates 37.1g | 12% |
| Dietary Fiber 6.1g | 24% |
| Sugars 4.3g | |
| Protein 26.7g | |

| Vitamin A 26% | • | Vitamin C 158% |
|---|---|---|
| Calcium 3% | • | Iron 24% |

Nutrition Grade B
* Based on a 2000 calorie diet

High in vitamin B12
Very high in vitamin C

YIELD:
Serves 4

NOTES:
You can use just about any kind of thinly sliced steak for this recipe. I have had success with everything from chuck to sirloin to flank.

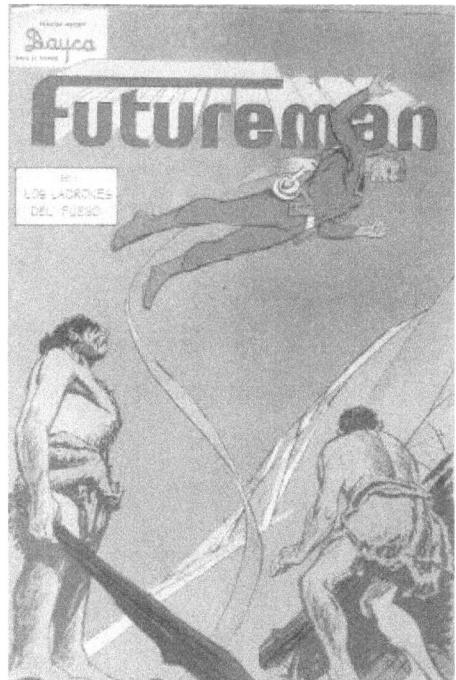

## SPACE WRECKED WOMEN ROASTED GARLIC BARLEY BEEF STEW

# ROASTED GARLIC BARLEY BEEF STEW

With a mellow accent of roasted garlic and the rich, nutty flavor of barley, it is best to make this stew well ahead of serving. If you have never cooked with barley, this stew is sure to make you a fan. Nothing beats a beef and barley stew on a cold day. Make a double batch so that you can freeze half of it for a quick, filling meal any time.

INGREDIENTS:

1 cup pearl barley, "picked over" and drained (see PREPARATION for more information)

2 pounds of lean, boneless beef chuck, trimmed and cut into 1-inch cubes

1 quart (about a liter) of beef stock (or beef broth)

1 head of fresh garlic (about 2 ounces)

5 TBS extra virgin olive oil, divided

1 medium yellow onion

3 medium carrots

2 medium green bell peppers

¼ cup dry red wine ① (see NOTES for possible substitute)

2 TBS tomato paste

dash/pinch salt (Kosher or sea salt is best) to taste

dash/pinch fresh ground black pepper to taste

SUPPLIES:

4 to 6 quart Dutch Oven

measuring cups/spoons

good sharp knife

cutting board

mixing bowls

Aluminum foil

Baking sheet or pie pan

Splatter screen

## PREPARATION:

For steps 1 and 3, preheat oven to 325° degrees F (165° degrees C).

1) Pour out your required cup of barley onto a cutting board or clean countertop and "pick over" the barley. Carefully check for and remove anything that isn't barley, especially small pebbles.

2) Soak the barley.

In mixing bowl, place the barley and enough warm water to cover by 3 inches. Soak for at least one hour then drain.

3) Roast the garlic.

Rub the head a bit in your hands and remove some of the papery outer sheath. Another technique is to place the head in an empty quart mason jar and shake it like a maraca.

Now slice the top $\frac{1}{4}$ inch off the top of the garlic exposing the tips of the individual cloves. Place the garlic in the middle of a 1 foot by 1 foot sheet of foil. Rub the bulb entirely with 1 tsp of extra virgin olive oil, then wrap tightly in the foil.

Place the wrapped garlic head on a baking sheet or pie pan and roast for about 1 hour or until the bulb is very soft when pierced with a fork. When cool enough to handle, break off the cloves and squeeze or press the cloves at the base to push the pulp out into a small bowl or ramekin. Using a fork, smash the pulp into a paste and reserve until ready to use. If keeping overnight, store in an airtight container in the refrigerator.

NOTE: You can easily perform steps 1 to 3 of the prep work to make this dish 1 to 2 days in advance.

4) When preparing to make the dish:

Let your beef reach room temperature and dry it completely.

Finely chop ⓘ the onion, carrot, and bell pepper.

If using a wine substitute ⓘ (see NOTES) mix and let stand.

If not already cubed, cut 2 pounds of lean, boneless beef chuck, trimmed and cut into 1-inch cubes.

If desired, lightly coat the beef cubes with extra virgin olive oil and any rub or your preferred seasonings other than salt.

## DIRECTIONS:

Heat 2 TBS of extra virgin olive oil in the Dutch oven over medium heat for 1 minute. In the Dutch oven, add beef cubes in batches of about a handful at a time, and sear, turning them often so that the cubes brown evenly on all sides. Sear for about 5 to 7 minutes per batch. When each batch is done, transfer to bowl and reserve before adding the next batch.

Do not remove anything or clean the Dutch oven once you have finished browning all the beef. Instead, immediately add the remaining 2 TBS of extra virgin olive oil and let heat for about 30 seconds then add onion, carrots, and bell pepper. Stirring often, cook over medium heat for 4 to 5 minutes or until the onion is tender but not browned.

Carefully pour in the beef stock (it's going to splatter - try pouring against the side of the pan). Stir in the reserved beef along with the wine (or substitute) until well mixed and then bring to a boil. Let boil for 1 minute.

Reduce heat to medium-low and stir in the drained barley. Simmer for 50 to 60 minutes, stirring occasionally, or until the meat is tender but not falling apart, and the barley is tender and triple its original size.

Stir in the tomato paste and reserved roasted garlic until well blended. Season to taste with salt and pepper.

Transfer to soup tureen and serve.

## NUTRITION:

| Nutrition Facts | |
|---|---|
| Serving Size 101 g | |
| **Amount Per Serving** | |
| Calories 122 | Calories from Fat 43 |
| | % Daily Value* |
| Total Fat 4.7g | 7% |
| Saturated Fat 1.2g | 6% |
| Trans Fat 0.0g | |
| Cholesterol 29mg | 10% |
| Sodium 144mg | 6% |
| Total Carbohydrates 8.0g | 3% |
| Dietary Fiber 1.6g | 7% |
| Sugars 1.1g | |
| Protein 11.3g | |
| Vitamin A 28% • | Vitamin C 21% |
| Calcium 1% • | Iron 36% |
| * Based on a 2000 calorie diet | |

Low in sugar

Very high in iron

High in selenium

Very high in vitamin A

Very high in vitamin B6

Very high in vitamin B12

High in vitamin C

High in zinc

**YIELD:**

About 6 to 8 large servings of hearty stew.

**NOTES:**

Try serving this wonderful, rich stew with homemade Sourdough or French bread or over rice.

I believe barley should be a key ingredient in most beef and lamb stews. The Whole Grain Council is a great resource for the health benefits of this wonderful, delicious grain.
http://wholegrainscouncil.org/whole-grains-101/health-benefits-of-barley

ⓘ If you abstain from alcohol even in cooking, you can substitute a 100% pure grape juice (ensure there is no apple juice in it) and one tsp of distilled vinegar to approximate the same flavor and properties while cooking.

ⓘ For information about a tip for chopping vegetables, follow this link:
http://www.halleethehomemaker.com/chopping-veg

## PIZZIAOLA SKILLET PHILLY STEAK & POTATOES

This wonderful traditional "meat and potatoes" recipe gets an added flair from the Italian flavors, making this incredible dish reminiscent of a traditional Pizziaola.

INGREDIENTS:

4 (6 ounce) sirloin strip steaks

4 TBS extra virgin olive oil, divided

2 medium diced tomatoes (or a 14.5 ounce can)

3 Red Bliss potatoes (about $^1/_2$ lbs diced in $^1/_2$ inch cubes)

1 yellow onion, coarsely chopped ⓘ

1 green bell pepper, cored, seeded, and thinly sliced

1 cup sliced cremini mushrooms

5 to 6 artichoke hearts (one 14 ounce can), drained and chopped

4 fresh garlic cloves, peeled, thinly sliced

2 tsp fresh chopped oregano (or 1 tsp dried)

2 tsp fresh chopped basil (or 1 tsp dried)

3 sprigs fresh lemon thyme, stripped and chopped (optional)

2 TBS capers

$^1/_8$ tsp red pepper flakes

1 TBS Montreal Steak seasoning mix

dash/pinch salt (Kosher or sea salt is best) to taste

dash/pinch fresh ground black pepper to taste

SUPPLIES:

12 inch seasoned skillet or Dutch oven

measuring cups/spoons

good sharp knife

cutting board

mixing bowl

mandolin (optional)

splatter screen (optional)

PREPARATION:

Preheat oven to 375° degrees F (190° degrees C).

Let your steaks fully reach room temperature and dry them completely with paper towels or clean kitchen towel.

Lightly coat steaks with extra virgin olive oil.

"Rub" the steaks evenly with Montreal Steak seasoning mix then reserve.

Coarsely chop ① onion.

Very thinly slice garlic.

Thinly slice bell pepper and mushrooms (mandolin is ideal for this).

Cube potatoes.

Chop fresh oregano, basil, lemon thyme.

DIRECTIONS:

Heat 2 TBS extra virgin olive oil over medium-high heat in a large 12" cast iron skillet.

When hot, add the steaks to sear. Brown for 5 minutes per side. You may want to use a splatter screen while browning.

Transfer steaks to a plate.

Add the remaining 2 TBS extra virgin olive oil to the skillet, and heat.

When hot, add the onion, potato, green pepper, mushrooms, chopped artichoke hearts, garlic, and capers.

Sauté for 6 to 8 minutes or until the onion is translucent and soft but not browned.

Add the diced tomato, oregano, basil, thyme, and red pepper, and stir to combine. Cook an additional 2 minutes.

Place the steaks on top of the tomato mixture and transfer to the middle rack of the hot oven. Bake for 20 minutes, remove, and serve hot.

NUTRITION:

| Nutrition Facts | |
|---|---|
| Serving Size 101 g | |
| **Amount Per Serving** | |
| Calories 311 | Calories from Fat 200 |
| | % Daily Value* |
| Total Fat 22.3g | 34% |
| Saturated Fat 8.8g | 44% |
| Cholesterol 76mg | 25% |
| Sodium 64mg | 3% |
| Total Carbohydrates 6.5g | 2% |
| Dietary Fiber 2.3g | 9% |
| Sugars 1.3g | |
| Protein 24.0g | |
| Vitamin A 39% • | Vitamin C 7% |
| Calcium 4% • | Iron 21% |
| * Based on a 2000 calorie diet | |

Low in sugar

Very high in vitamin B6

Very high in iron

High in vitamin A

High in vitamin C

YIELD:

4 adult servings.

NOTES:

ⓘ For information about a tip for chopping vegetables, follow this link: http://www.halleethehomemaker.com/chopping-veg

## MOROCCAN STYLE SKIRT STEAK WITH ROASTED RED PEPPER COUSCOUS

Thin cuts of beef, such as skirt or flank steak, cook very quickly when seared in a hot cast iron skillet and that kind of time-saver is just right for a busy weeknight. You will love how the spicy Moroccan flavors on the steak complement the sweet, roasted pepper-studded couscous.

### INGREDIENTS:

1 lbs skirt or flank (see NOTES) or sirloin, cut $^3/_4$ to 1 inch thick, trimmed

1 TBS plus 1 tsp extra virgin olive oil, divided

$^2/_3$ cup whole wheat couscous

2 medium red bell peppers

2 TBS chopped green olives

1 tsp ground coriander

1 tsp ground cumin

$^1/_2$ tsp ground turmeric

$^1/_2$ tsp ground cinnamon

$^1/_2$ tsp freshly ground black pepper

$^3/_4$ tsp salt (Kosher or sea salt is best)

1 whole lemon and additional lemon wedges for garnish

### SUPPLIES:

10 to 12 inch diameter cast iron skillet

good sharp knife

cutting board

measuring cups/spoons

bowls and/or ramekins

citrus zester/juicer

baking sheet

small saucepan and cover

## PREPARATION:

Roast the red bell peppers ①:

Position rack in upper third of oven and preheat oven on broil, or bring to about 500° degrees F (260° degrees C).

Place peppers on a baking sheet and roast under the broiler about 10 to 15 minutes until charred and softened, turning every 5 minutes. Place in brown paper bag and let cool. Transfer to a clean cutting board. Peel the peppers and slice into strips.

Combine coriander, cumin, turmeric, cinnamon, and pepper in ramekin.

Grate $1/2$ tsp lemon zest then juice lemon into a measuring cup. Add water to make 1 full cup.

## DIRECTIONS:

Pour lemon juice and water into small saucepan then add the lemon zest, 1 tsp of the spice mixture, $1/4$ tsp Kosher salt, and 1 tsp of extra virgin olive oil.

Bring to a boil. Stir in couscous.

Cover and remove from heat. Let stand while you prepare the rest of the meal.

Rub the remaining spice mixture on both sides of steak.

Heat the remaining 1 TBS extra virgin olive oil in cast iron skillet over medium heat until just shimmering but not smoking.

Cook the steak 2 to 3 minutes per side for medium-rare turning only once. Let rest on the cutting board for 5 minutes.

Stir olives and the peppers into the couscous. Thinly slice the steak and serve with the couscous and lemon wedges, if desired.

 YIELD:

About 4 servings

NUTRITION:

| Nutrition Facts | | |
|---|---|---|
| Serving Size 101 g | | |
| **Amount Per Serving** | | |
| Calories 177 | | Calories from Fat 54 |
| | | % Daily Value* |
| Total Fat 6.0g | | 9% |
| Saturated Fat 1.5g | | 8% |
| Trans Fat 0.0g | | |
| Cholesterol 45mg | | 15% |
| Sodium 245mg | | 10% |
| Total Carbohydrates 13.3g | | 4% |
| Dietary Fiber 2.2g | | 9% |
| Sugars 1.5g | | |
| Protein 18.0g | | |
| Vitamin A 17% | • | Vitamin C 61% |
| Calcium 2% | • | Iron 57% |
| * Based on a 2000 calorie diet | | |

Low in sugar

Very high in iron

High in selenium

Very high in vitamin B6

Very high in vitamin B12

Very high in vitamin C

High in zinc

NOTES:

Skirt steak or flank steak is often also referred to as fajita steak in Hispanic cultures. It is a thin, flavorful, and relatively inexpensive cut of beef. Look for it in well-stocked supermarkets or ask your butcher to order it for you. If it isn't available, sirloin will substitute.

I have included a good Red Meat Marinade recipe in this cookbook. You may want to tenderize and marinate this steak well in advance of preparing this dish for an even more unique and flavorful experience.

ⓘ for information how to roast red peppers, go to this link:
http://www.halleethehomemaker.com/roasted-peppers

## SKILLET ZITI                    ❄ ⏱ 🌐 🍽

Baked ziti is one of my favorite meals. But this ziti in a skillet is so creamy and so cheesy, it will easily become a regular meal in your house.

### INGREDIENTS:

1 lbs beef round, ground

2 cans (or 1 large can) organic stewed tomatoes, with the juice

3 small cans organic tomato sauce

1 small can organic tomato paste

2 Tbs olive oil

1 medium onion, chopped ⓘ

3 cloves garlic, finely diced

$^1/_2$ tablespoon salt, kosher or sea salt is best

1 teaspoon black pepper

2 tablespoons brown sugar or honey

1 tablespoon dried oregano

1 tablespoon dried parsley

2 teaspoons dried basil

1 teaspoon dried sage

1 bay leaf

8 ounces uncooked ziti

1 cup plain yogurt (or sour cream)

$^1/_2$ cup Parmesan cheese, shredded

$^1/_4$ cup Mozzarella cheese, shredded

$^1/_4$ cup Provolone cheese, shredded

$^1/_4$ cup Romano cheese, shredded

$^1/_4$ cup Fontina cheese, shredded

$^1/_4$ cup Asiago cheese, shredded

**SUPPLIES:**

Large cast iron skillet with lid

pasta pan

sauce pan

spoons/ladles

clean cutting board for meat

good sharp knife

cheese grater

**PREPARATION:**

Grate the cheeses. Keep the Parmesan cheese separate.

Dice the onion and garlic.

**DIRECTIONS:**

Brown hamburger meat in skillet until brown. Add onion. Cook until tender.
Add diced garlic. Cook about 5 minutes longer.

Add tomatoes, tomato sauce, and tomato paste. Stir in salt, black pepper, brown sugar (or honey), oregano, parsley, basil, sage, and the bay leaf.

Bring to a boil, then reduce heat to low, cover, and simmer for at least 1 hour, stirring regularly. The longer it simmers, the more the spices have a chance to infuse the sauce.

After about an hour, taste it and see if it needs more sugar, or more salt, or a touch more oregano. Let your tongue guide you.

Add a little bit at a time, give it a few minutes to blend in with the flavors, then taste it again. (A good way to taste is to dip a bit of bread in it.)

Cook pasta according to package directions. Drain. Stir into pasta sauce.

Combine sour cream and Parmesan cheese. Stir into pasta mixture. Sprinkle Italian cheese blend over pasta mixture. Cover, reduce heat to medium, and cook 5 minutes or until cheese melts.

YIELD:

Serves: 8

NUTRITION:

## Nutrition Facts

Very high in vitamin B6

Serving Size 331 g

| Amount Per Serving | |
| --- | --- |
| Calories 502 | Calories from Fat 232 |
| | % Daily Value* |
| Total Fat 25.8g | 40% |
| Saturated Fat 12.4g | 62% |
| Trans Fat 0.5g | |
| Cholesterol 81mg | 27% |
| Sodium 1193mg | 50% |
| Potassium 486mg | 14% |
| Total Carbohydrates 37.0g | 12% |
| Dietary Fiber 3.8g | 15% |
| Sugars 11.5g | |
| Protein 31.9g | |

| | | | |
| --- | --- | --- | --- |
| Vitamin A 31% | • | Vitamin C 35% | |
| Calcium 48% | • | Iron 19% | |

NOTES:

ⓘ For information about a tip for chopping vegetables, follow this link: http://www.halleethehomemaker.com/chopping-veg

## ITALIAN GROUND BEEF SKILLET ✳ ⏱ 🌐 📷

This is a quick pasta sauce that every member of our family will love. The kale is a wonderful source of vitamins A, C, and K, as well as omega 3 and omega 6. You can use any kind of pasta you want when making this dish. It takes very little time to make, and using grass-fed beef and organic vegetables it's still barely $3 per person.

INGREDIENTS:

1 pound grass-fed beef

1 TBS Italian seasoning

1 medium onion

1 green bell pepper

8 oil-packed sundried tomatoes

1 15-ounce can diced tomatoes

1 bunch lacinato kale

2 tsp chopped garlic

1 pound whole wheat pasta

SUPPLIES:

sharp knife/cutting board

measuring cups/spoons

skillet

pot and colander

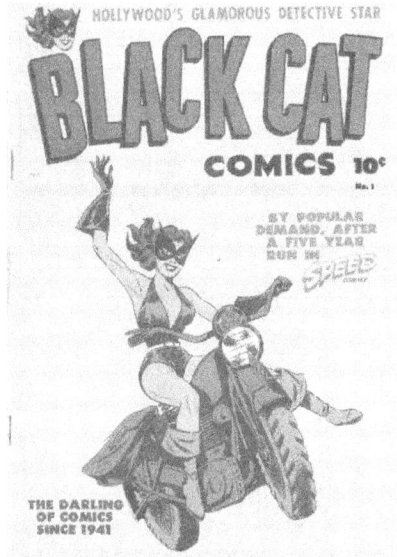

PREPARATION:

Prepare the pasta according to the package instructions.

Chop the onion, green pepper, and garlic. ①

Slice the tomatoes in very thin slices.

Slice the kale, removing the tough stems.

DIRECTIONS:

Brown beef with the Italian seasoning, onion, green pepper, and the oil-packed sundried tomatoes.

Add the diced tomatoes, kale, and chopped garlic.

Toss with the cooked and drained pasta.

NUTRITION:

| Nutrition Facts | |
|---|---|
| Serving Size 443 g | |

| Amount Per Serving | |
|---|---|
| Calories 717 | Calories from Fat 146 |
| | % Daily Value* |
| Total Fat 16.2g | 25% |
| Saturated Fat 5.0g | 25% |
| Trans Fat 0.0g | |
| Cholesterol 77mg | 26% |
| Sodium 154mg | 6% |
| Potassium 1015mg | 29% |
| Total Carbohydrates 99.6g | 33% |
| Dietary Fiber 13.8g | 55% |
| Sugars 9.5g | |
| Protein 40.2g | |
| Vitamin A 145% • Vitamin C 183% | |
| Calcium 12% • Iron 51% | |
| Nutrition Grade B+ | |
| * Based on a 2000 calorie diet | |

Low in sodium
High in vitamin A
Very high in vitamin B6
Very high in vitamin C

YIELD:

Serves: 4

NOTES:

ⓘ For information about a tip for chopping vegetables, follow this link:
http://www.halleethehomemaker.com/chopping-veg

Don't use extra virgin olive oil to season or clean your cast iron. Use cold pressed organic flaxseed oil if possible.

IRON SKILLET MAN SAYS...

# IRISH GROUND BEEF SKILLET ❄ ⏱ 🌐 🍽

This is an easy, quick skillet dinner that provides a different taste than the normal macaroni casserole. It is also extremely affordable – $3.73 per serving.

**INGREDIENTS:**

1 lb. lean ground grass-fed beef

1 medium onion

$^1/_2$ cup lager or pilsner beer

2 cups sliced organic green cabbage

4 large potatoes

2 cups shredded cheddar cheese

**SUPPLIES:**

sharp knife/cutting board

skillet

measuring cups/spoons

**PREPARATION:**

Chop onion. ①

Slice cabbage in thin strips.

Shred cheese.

Bake potatoes.

**DIRECTIONS:**

In a skillet over medium-high heat, brown the beef with the onion.

Add the beer. Add the cabbage and cook until cabbage wilts.

Spoon over the baked potatoes and top each with $^1/_4$ cup grated cheddar cheese.

**YIELD:**

Serves: 4

NUTRITION:

| Nutrition Facts | |
| --- | --- |
| Serving Size 631 g | |
| **Amount Per Serving** | |
| Calories 716 | Calories from Fat 262 |
| | % Daily Value* |
| Total Fat 29.1g | 45% |
| Saturated Fat 16.5g | 83% |
| Cholesterol 134mg | 45% |
| Sodium 456mg | 19% |
| Potassium 1665mg | 48% |
| Total Carbohydrates 64.3g | 21% |
| Dietary Fiber 10.3g | 41% |
| Sugars 6.8g | |
| Protein 44.1g | |
| Vitamin A 13% • | Vitamin C 149% |
| Calcium 48% • | Iron 29% |

High in vitamin A
Very high in vitamin C

NOTES:

ⓘ For information about a tip for chopping vegetables, follow this link:
http://www.halleethehomemaker.com/chopping-veg

## QUICK & EASY SLOPPY JOES　❋ ⏱ ✡ 🍲

My dad came up with this recipe one time. My mom was somewhere doing something and Daddy had to make dinner. He browned hamburger then started dumping things into the pan. He used home canned tomatoes and home canned green beans, which made his version amazing. I've not enjoyed Sloppy Joes without the green veggie since.

### INGREDIENTS:

| | |
|---|---|
| 1 pound lean grass-fed ground beef | 1 small onion |
| 1 15-ounce can diced tomatoes | 1 small green pepper |
| 1 8-ounce can tomato sauce | 1 clove garlic |
| 1 tsp salt (Kosher or sea salt is best) | $^1/_2$ tsp dried basil |
| $^1/_2$ tsp fresh ground black pepper | |

1 can or 1 cup fresh or frozen green beans

Homemade Whole Wheat Hamburger Buns ⓘ

### SUPPLIES:

| | |
|---|---|
| skillet | measuring cups/spoons |
| sharp knife and cutting board | wooden spoon |
| garlic mincer | |

### PREPARATION:

Dice onion and green pepper. ⓘ

Mince (or finely chop) garlic.

Cook green beans if using fresh.

### DIRECTIONS:

Place ground beef in skillet. Add onion, green pepper, and garlic. Cook until beef is browned and onion is tender. Add salt, pepper, basil, tomatoes (undrained), tomato sauce, add green beans.

Stir well. Cook over medium heat until thoroughly hot.

Split hamburger bun. Top with Sloppy Joe mix.

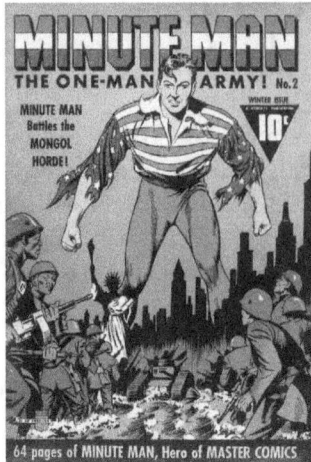

64 pages of MINUTE MAN, Hero of MASTER COMICS

NUTRITION:

## Nutrition Facts

Serving Size 101 g

**Amount Per Serving**

| Calories 96 | Calories from Fat 22 |
|---|---|
| | **% Daily Value*** |
| **Total Fat** 2.4g | **4%** |
| Saturated Fat 0.8g | **4%** |
| **Cholesterol** 27mg | **9%** |
| **Sodium** 291mg | **12%** |
| **Total Carbohydrates** 8.1g | **3%** |
| Dietary Fiber 1.7g | **7%** |
| Sugars 2.6g | |
| **Protein** 10.7g | |

| Vitamin A 7% | • | Vitamin C 17% |
|---|---|---|
| Calcium 2% | • | Iron 9% |

**Nutrition Grade A**

* Based on a 2000 calorie diet

High in manganese
High in niacin
High in phosphorus
Very high in selenium
High in vitamin B6
High in vitamin B12
High in vitamin C
High in zinc

YIELD:

4 servings

NOTES:

ⓘ For information about a tip for chopping vegetables, follow this link:
http://www.halleethehomemaker.com/chopping-veg

ⓘ For a wonderful Whole Wheat Hamburger Bun recipe, follow this link:
http://www.halleethehomemaker.com/burger-buns

## CAJUN GROUND BEEF SKILLET     ✳ ⏱ ✡ 🔥 🍲

This is a wonderful recipe with a hint of kick. If you have preprepared rice, it's a quick fix. But remember – the rice will take 45 minutes to cook so try to plan ahead a little bit.

**INGREDIENTS:**

1 lb. lean ground grass-fed ground beef

4 tsp salt & MSG-free Cajun/Creole seasoning (divided 1 $\frac{1}{2}$ tsp, 1 $\frac{1}{2}$ tsp, and 1 tsp) ⓘ

1 medium onion, chopped ⓘ

2 celery stalks, chopped ⓘ

1 sweet red bell pepper, chopped ⓘ

1 can (15 oz.) rinsed and drained kidney beans

4 cups cooked Perfect Brown Rice ⓘ

**SUPPLIES:**

large skillet

sharp knife/cutting board

measuring cups/spoons

**PREPARATION:**

Chop the onion. Thinly slice the celery and the bell pepper.

Prepare the rice.

If necessary, whip up a batch of homemade Cajun/Creole seasoning

**DIRECTIONS:**

Brown beef with 1 $\frac{1}{2}$ tsp Cajun/Creole seasoning.

Add onion, celery, bell pepper, and another 1 $\frac{1}{2}$ tsp Cajun/Creole seasoning. Cook until the veggies are tender.

Toss with 4 cups cooked brown rice, rinsed and drained kidney beans, and 1 more tsp of the Cajun/Creole seasoning.

Heat through, then let cool for a few minutes before you serve.

**YIELD:**

4 servings

NUTRITION:

| Nutrition Facts | | |
|---|---|---|
| Serving Size 100 g | | |
| Amount Per Serving | | |
| Calories 268 | Calories from Fat 31 | |
| | % Daily Value* | |
| Total Fat 3.5g | | 5% |
| Saturated Fat 1.2g | | 6% |
| Cholesterol 16mg | | 5% |
| Sodium 22mg | | 1% |
| Total Carbohydrates 45.3g | | 15% |
| Dietary Fiber 5.1g | | 20% |
| Sugars 1.0g | | |
| Protein 13.0g | | |
| Vitamin A 6% | • | Vitamin C 16% |
| Calcium 4% | • | Iron 16% |
| * Based on a 2000 calorie diet | | |

Very low in sodium

Low in saturated fat

Low in cholesterol

Low in sugar

High in vitamin B6

Very high in manganese

NOTES:

I have included a recipe for a really good salt-free and MSG-free Cajun/Creole seasoning in this cookbook. I recommend it for this recipe.

ⓘ For information about a tip for chopping vegetables, follow this link: http://www.halleethehomemaker.com/chopping-veg

ⓘ For tips to cook perfect brown rice, follow this link: http://www.halleethehomemaker.com/brown-rice/

## PHANTOM LADY TACO MEAT

**TASTY TACO MEAT**

This is a wonderful base recipe to make anything from tacos to burritos to taco salad to nachos. It's flavorful, and you can control the level of spice and seasoning to suit your own tastes.

INGREDIENTS:

1 lb of ground meat (beef, turkey, venison)

1 small onion

1 can diced green chillies

1 tsp ground cumin

$^1/_2$ tsp chili powder

$^1/_2$ tsp salt (Kosher or sea salt is best)

$^1/_4$ tsp fresh ground black pepper

SUPPLIES:

skillet                          colander

sharp knife                      measuring cups/spoons

cutting board                    wooden spoon

PREPARATION:

Dice onion. ⓘ

DIRECTIONS:

Put ground meat and onion in frying pan.

Cook over medium heat until the meat is browned and cooked through.

Drain.  Do not drain your meat in your sink.  I drain mine into a heavy ceramic bowl and allow it to cool before putting it in the garbage can.

Add the diced green chilies and the spices.

Cook and stir until thoroughly heated.

YIELD:

Serves: 4

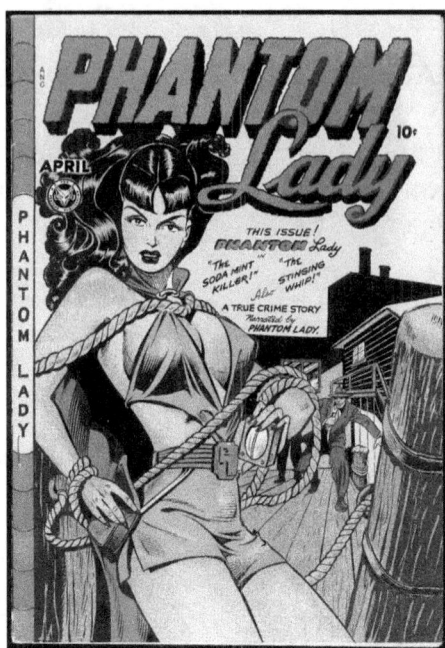

NUTRITION:

## Nutrition Facts

Serving Size 108 g

Amount Per Serving

| Calories 154 | Calories from Fat 43 |
|---|---|
| | % Daily Value* |
| Total Fat 4.8g | 7% |
| Saturated Fat 1.8g | 9% |
| Cholesterol 68mg | 23% |
| Sodium 249mg | 10% |
| Potassium 333mg | 10% |
| Total Carbohydrates 2.8g | 1% |
| Sugars 1.2g | |
| Protein 23.1g | |

| Vitamin A 1% | • | Vitamin C 3% |
|---|---|---|
| Calcium 1% | • | Iron 81% |

Nutrition Grade B+

* Based on a 2000 calorie diet

High in manganese
High in niacin
High in phosphorus
Very high in selenium
High in vitamin B6
High in vitamin B12
High in vitamin C
High in zinc

NOTES:

ⓘ For information about a tip for chopping vegetables, follow this link:
http://www.halleethehomemaker.com/chopping-veg

# FIESTA CUBED STEAK  ❄ ⏱ ✡ ⚗ 🌐 🍽

The chillies and cilantro give this cubed steak skillet dish a wonderful kick. Serve with rice to make a meal that will become a new family favorite.

**INGREDIENTS:**

4 (6 oz) beef cubed steaks

1 cup Hallee's Bodacious Beef Broth ⓘ

$^1/_4$ cup filtered water

$^1/_4$ cup flour (I use fresh ground soft white wheat)

1 TBS extra virgin olive oil

2 TBS cornstarch

1 $^3/_4$ cup diced tomatoes (See NOTES)

4 TBS diced green chilies (See NOTES)

$^1/_2$ tsp paprika

$^1/_4$ tsp fresh ground black pepper

1 TBS fresh chopped cilantro

**SUPPLIES:**

large skillet

measuring cups/spoons

sharp knife and cutting board

sturdy tongs/spoon

Shallow plate or bowl for dredging steaks in flour

**PREPARATION:**

Chop the cilantro.

**DIRECTIONS:**

In a shallow dish, combine flour, paprika, and pepper; add steaks and turn to coat lightly.

In large skillet, heat olive oil over medium-high heat. Add the steaks. Cook 10 to 14 minutes, turning halfway through cooking.

Remove steaks from skillet and cover to keep warm. Reduce heat to medium and add broth and diced tomatoes to skillet.

Heat, stirring occasionally, just until mixture begins to boil.

In a small bowl, combine water and cornstarch; stir until smooth.

Slowly stir cornstarch mixture into tomato mixture and stir until thickened and smooth. Return steaks to pan and cook until thoroughly heated. Sprinkle with cilantro and serve immediately.

YIELD:

Serves 4

NUTRITION:

| Nutrition Facts | | |
|---|---|---|
| Serving Size 329 g | | |
| Amount Per Serving | | |
| Calories 389 | Calories from Fat 160 | |
| | | % Daily Value* |
| Total Fat 17.8g | | 27% |
| Saturated Fat 5.9g | | 30% |
| Cholesterol 68mg | | 23% |
| Sodium 295mg | | 12% |
| Total Carbohydrates 14.2g | | 5% |
| Dietary Fiber 1.8g | | 7% |
| Sugars 2.9g | | |
| Protein 40.5g | | |
| Vitamin A 26% | • | Vitamin C 17% |
| Calcium 1% | • | Iron 25% |

High in niacin
High in vitamin A
High in vitamin B6

NOTES:

You can substitute a 14.5 oz undrained can of diced tomatoes with chilies for the tomatoes and chilis in this recipe.

ⓘ I have included a recipe for Hallee's Bodacious Beef Broth in this cookbook. If you don't have stock on hand, be sure to use a good organic stock with low or no salt.

## Top Cuts!

As I said before, A perfectly seared, perfectly cooked, medium-rare one inch thick prime top cut need not be the centerpiece of every meal.

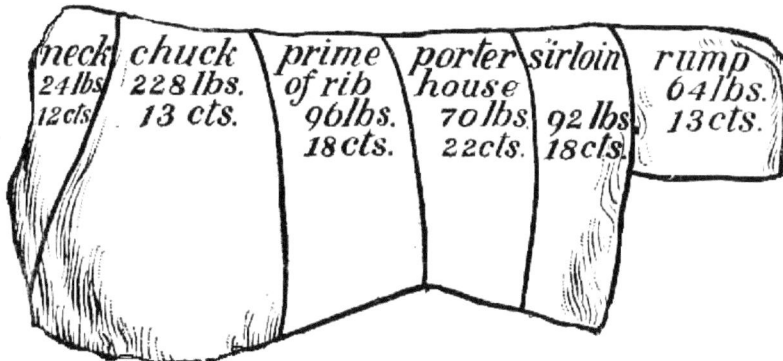

| neck | chuck | prime of rib | porter house | sirloin | rump |
|------|-------|--------------|--------------|---------|------|
| 24 lbs 12 cts | 228 lbs. 13 cts. | 96 lbs. 18 cts. | 70 lbs. 22 cts. | 92 lbs 18 cts. | 64 lbs. 13 cts. |

But when it can be – oh, my is it a great and wonderful thing!

These are the kinds of meals that family members talk about for weeks or months or even years to come.

Never let cast iron cookware "air dry". Any moisture left on cast iron can cause rust. Thoroughly dry it with a towel and set it on a warm burner or in a hot oven with a light coat of oil for a few minutes after cleaning. Store cast iron in the oven to prevent rusting. It works better in gas stoves with pilot lights that keep the moisture out of the air.

IRON SKILLET MAN SAYS...

## DUTCH OVEN ROAST     ❄ ✡ 🍬 🪶 🌐 🍷 🍲 🍽

Roast beef is a comfort food of mine. This recipe is cooked in a Dutch oven or roasting pan. Accompanied by different vegetables, this pot roast is a one-pot meal. Use either a bone-in or boneless roast. I personally prefer bone-in for the added flavor to the broth.

### INGREDIENTS:

8 pound chuck roast, 2 to 3 inches thick, bone in if available

$^1/_2$ cup Burgundy wine ⓘ (see NOTES for substitute)

2 cups warm water

$^1/_4$ cup extra virgin olive oil

$^1/_4$ cup Montreal Steak seasoning mix ⓘ

6 carrots

3 yellow onions

2 cloves garlic

$^1/_2$ cup baby bella mushrooms

3 TBS cornstarch

$^1/_2$ cup water

### SUPPLIES:

4 to 6 quart Dutch Oven          cutting board
measuring cups/spoons          mixing bowls
good sharp knife                      splatter screen

### PREPARATION:

Cut carrots into chunks.          Dice the garlic.
Cut onions into wedges.          Slice the mushrooms.

### DIRECTIONS:

Heat extra virgin olive oil in a 12 qt. camp Dutch oven.

Lightly coat chuck roast with extra virgin olive oil then rub with $^1/_4$ cup

Montreal Steak seasoning mix. Sear on all sides in the hot oil.

Pour warm water and Burgundy wine over roast. Add garlic, onions, carrots and sliced mushrooms.

Cover and cook about 2 $^1/_2$ hours, turning every 30 to 45 minutes. Pour cooking liquid into a large measuring cup. Skim away fat. If necessary, add a little water or red wine to make 4 cups liquid and return to the cooking pan.

Stir in the cornstarch dissolved in $^1/_2$ cup water. Bring to a boil, reduce heat and simmer for 3 minutes.

Return roast to cooking pan and arrange vegetables around the roast. Cover and allow to rest 15 minutes before serving. Lightly salt if desired.

YIELD:

14 to 16 Servings

NUTRITION:

| Nutrition Facts | | |
|---|---|---|
| Serving Size 100 g | | |
| **Amount Per Serving** | | |
| Calories 171 | | Calories from Fat 62 |
| | | % Daily Value* |
| Total Fat 6.8g | | 11% |
| Saturated Fat 2.2g | | 11% |
| *Trans* Fat 0.0g | | |
| Cholesterol 70mg | | 23% |
| Sodium 52mg | | 2% |
| Total Carbohydrates 2.4g | | 1% |
| Dietary Fiber 0.6g | | 2% |
| Sugars 0.8g | | |
| Protein 23.3g | | |
| Vitamin A 27% | • | Vitamin C 3% |
| Calcium 1% | • | Iron 16% |
| * Based on a 2000 calorie diet | | |

Low in sodium

Low in sugar

High in phosphorus

High in selenium

High in vitamin A

Very high in vitamin B6

Very high in vitamin B12

Very high in zinc

NOTES:

① If you abstain from alcohol even in cooking, you can substitute a 100% pure grape juice (ensure there is no apple juice in it) and one tsp of distilled vinegar to approximate the same flavor and properties while cooking.

① I have included the recipe for homemade Montreal Steak seasoning mix in this cookbook.

## OVEN SKILLET STEAK     ❄ ⏱ ✡ 🌾

This is an absolutely foolproof, quick and easy, and simple way to prepare a perfect steak indoors, in the oven. No propane grill or charcoal briquets required. This method takes 15 minutes, tops. It turns out a beautifully juicy, medium-rare steak with crisped and crunchy edges, and so much flavor you will simply feel amazed!

Add fresh baked bread, salad, baked potato, and something to wash it all down and you have an easy and delicious meal.

### INGREDIENTS:

A single lean ribeye steak, cut 1 to 1 ½ inches thick and about 1 pound in weight (boneless or bone-in makes no difference, though I prefer the flavor of bone-in)

extra virgin olive oil to coat (grapeseed oil, butter, or tallow can substitute)

1 TBS Montreal Steak seasoning mix ①

## (OPTIONAL) SKILLET SAUCE REDUCTION     ❄ ⏱ ✡ 🌾 🍷

½ cup of beef (or chicken) stock

½ cup of Cabernet or other dry red wine ① (see NOTES for substitute)

### SUPPLIES:

10 to 12 inch diameter cast iron skillet

long sturdy kitchen tongs

Very thick, well-padded oven mitt or pad

bowls and/or ramekins

basting brush

timer or egg timer

whisk

### PREPARATION:

Place the 10 to 12 inch diameter cast iron skillet in the oven. With the skillet inside, set the oven to broil, or bring to about 500° degrees F (260° degrees C).

Let your steaks fully reach room temperature and dry them completely with paper towels or clean kitchen towel.

DIRECTIONS:

1) While waiting for the oven and skillet to reach full heat, reserve about 2 TBS little extra virgin olive oil in a small bowl or ramekin. Mix in a generous amount of Montreal Steak seasoning mix.

Brush the oil all over the steak, coating it generously on both sides and on the ends. Once fully coated, generously "rub" the steaks evenly with Montreal Steak seasoning mix covering both sides of the steak, patting it into each steak so that it sticks.

2) When the oven with the skillet has reached broil, turn on a stove burner to High heat.

Using your thickest and most reliable oven mitt or pad, very carefully remove the piping hot cast iron skillet from the oven and place it on the High heat burner.

Use long, sturdy kitchen tongs and place your steak into the center of the hot pan. It should sizzle immediately.

Cook the steak for 30 seconds on one side, then flip it over. Cook the steak for an additional 30 seconds on the other side.

Turn off your burner. Immediately, and once again using your thickest and most reliable oven mitt or pad, carefully place the skillet with the seared steak in the middle back in the oven.

3) Using a timer if needed:

For a perfect MEDIUM-RARE steak, broil the steak in the skillet in the center of the hot oven for exactly 2 minutes. Open the oven and quickly but carefully flip the steak onto the other side using the long, sturdy kitchen tongs. Close the oven and cook for an additional 2 minutes.

For a perfect MEDIUM steak, add just 1 minute to the cooking time for each side for a total of 3 minutes per side instead of 2 minutes.

Turn off the oven and immediately, using your thickest and most reliable oven mitt or pad, quickly but carefully remove the steak from the oven. Using the tongs, remove the steak from the skillet and place it on a large cutting board. Cover with aluminum foil and let the steak rest for about 5 minutes before serving.

Serving suggestions:

There are three nice ways to serve this steak:

a) You can serve the steak on a serving tray and let your best carver slice and serve directly at the table.

b) You can slice and serve in a lovely presentation of fanned slices either on a serving platter or directly onto each plate next to attractive side items.

c) You can do either of the above with the addition of a heavenly skillet sauce reduction either served in a gravy boat with a ladle or poured directly over the sliced steak just at serving time.

While the steak is resting, you can whip up a delicious skillet sauce with the steak drippings still in the pan in no time. Bring a burner to medium heat. Put the skillet over the medium heat burner and add about $^1/_2$ cup of beef stock and about $^1/_2$ cup of red wine ① to the skillet.

Scrape up any small bits of steak still clinging to the skillet and whisk until well mixed. Bring to a boil then lower heat and simmer until the liquid volume is reduced by at least half, whisking occasionally.

Once the steak has rested, and just before carving, you may add a dash of Kosher salt to taste. Then, either let your best carver slice and serve directly at the table, or, using a very sharp knife, slice the steak against the grain.

Slice into $^1/_4$ inch to $^1/_2$ inch thick strips. Fan these slices out onto your serving platter or onto each individual plate next to your side items.

If you made the optional skillet sauce reduction, either pour into a gravy boat if carving your steak at the table, or, pour the reduced sauce directly over the sliced steak in a nice drizzle just before serving.

Serve immediately.

YIELD:

1 perfect steak to serve 2 to 4 adults.

NUTRITION:

| Nutrition Facts | |
|---|---|
| Serving Size 92 g | |
| **Amount Per Serving** | |
| Calories 314 | Calories from Fat 247 |
| | % Daily Value* |
| Total Fat 27.4g | 42% |
| Saturated Fat 11.4g | 57% |
| Cholesterol 64mg | 21% |
| Sodium 126mg | 5% |
| Total Carbohydrates 0.1g | 0% |
| Protein 15.3g | |
| Vitamin A 0% • | Vitamin C 0% |
| Calcium 0% • | Iron 8% |
| * Based on a 2000 calorie diet | |

Very high in protein

High in vitamin B12

No sugar

Low in sodium

NOTES:

① If you abstain from alcohol even in cooking, you can substitute a 100% pure grape juice (ensure there is no apple juice in it) and one tsp of distilled vinegar to approximate the same flavor and properties while cooking.

① I have included the recipe for homemade Montreal Steak seasoning mix in this cookbook.

## CABERNET FILET MIGNON

Filet mignon is such a wonderful cut of beef. If you cook it properly, it will be so tender that it will almost melt in your mouth. This steak, seasoned with the perfect flavors, and complimented with a butter and red wine reduction, is so amazing. This recipe is a real knock-out!

### INGREDIENTS:

4 Filet Mignon steaks about 4 to 5 ounces each cut $^3/_4$ inch to 1 inch thick (Beef Tenderloin)

2 TBS extra virgin olive oil, plus extra to lightly coat the steaks

1 TBS Montreal Steak seasoning mix ①

$^1/_2$ cup Cabernet or any good dry red wine ① (see NOTES for substitute)

2 TBS butter

### SUPPLIES:

oven-proof skillet

Measuring cups/spoons

Wooden spoon

### PREPARATION:

Let your steaks fully reach room temperature and dry them completely with paper towels or clean kitchen towel.

If roast-searing, with 10 to 12 inch diameter cast iron skillet inside, set the oven to broil, or bring to about 500° degrees F (260° degrees C).

### DIRECTIONS:

Lightly coat steaks with extra virgin olive oil. Rub 1 TBS Montreal Steak seasoning mix evenly over the steak (press in with your hands); set aside until ready to cook.

There are two methods you can employ to cook these knock-out steaks:

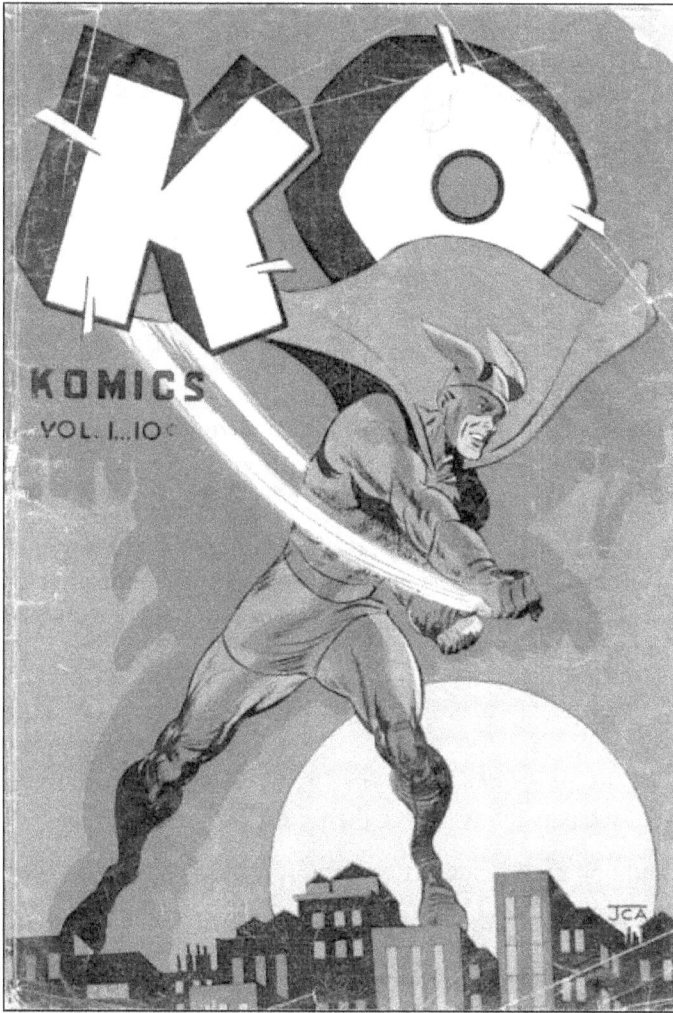

## 1) THE PAN-SEAR TECHNIQUE:

In a cast iron frying pan over medium-high heat, heat 2 TBS extra virgin olive oil just until shimmering, not smoking.

If you like, lightly coat the steaks with extra virgin olive oil and preferred seasonings.

Sear the steaks, moving them with tongs a little so they don't stick to the bottom, approximately 2 to 3 minutes per side turning twice. Cook steak to your desired doneness. Check for doneness with an electronic thermometer (See NOTES).

## 2) THE ROAST-SEAR TECHNIQUE:

A very hot oven produces a juicy interior. Preheat oven on broil, about 500 degrees F. If you like, lightly coat the steaks with extra virgin olive oil and preferred seasonings.

Place a 10- to 12-inch ovenproof skillet or cast-iron skillet in oven. When oven reaches desired temperature, remove skillet from oven and place on range over high heat. Be extremely careful – the skillet handle will be extremely hot.

Immediately place steaks in the middle of hot, dry pan. If cooking more than one piece of meat, add the steaks carefully so that they do not touch each other. Sear the steaks, cooking 30 seconds to 1 minute without moving. Turn with tongs and cook another 30 seconds to 1 minute turning them just this once.

Now place the cast iron skillet with the steaks inside into the center of the hot oven. Cook an additional 3 to 5 minutes, depending on thickness of steaks and degree of doneness you prefer. Cook to your desired doneness. Check for doneness with an electronic thermometer (See NOTES).

MAKING CABERNET WINE SAUCE:

Add the wine to the pan and bring to a boil, scraping any pieces of steak off the bottom of the pan and whisking them into the emerging sauce.

Let the liquid boil until reduced to approximately $1/3$ cup.

Remove pan from heat. Add the butter and mix it in by swirling the pan.

WHEN SUFFICIENTLY COOKED:

Using either of the above methods, When the steaks are crusty-charred and done to your liking, remove from heat entirely and place on a clean, cool dish such as a casserole dish, to catch any juices.

Cover loosely with aluminum foil, and let rest at least 5 to 10 minutes before serving.

During this time the meat will continue to cook. The meat temperature will rise anywhere from 5 to 10 degrees after it is removed from the heat and the juices will redistribute. Before moving your steak to a serving platter, add the juices that accumulated from the resting steaks to the Cabernet Wine Sauce and whisk.

Serve whole or slice thin and fan onto individual serving plates.

Pour the Cabernet Wine Sauce over your perfectly cooked steaks just before serving.

NUTRITION:

| Nutrition Facts | |
|---|---|
| Serving Size 104 g | |

| Amount Per Serving | |
|---|---|
| Calories 156 | Calories from Fat 49 |
| | % Daily Value* |
| Total Fat 5.4g | 8% |
| Saturated Fat 1.5g | 8% |
| Trans Fat 0.0g | |
| Cholesterol 31mg | 10% |
| Sodium 130mg | 5% |
| Total Carbohydrates 7.3g | 2% |
| Sugars 1.1g | |
| Protein 13.4g | |

| Vitamin A 1% | • | Vitamin C 1% |
|---|---|---|
| Calcium 2% | • | Iron 6% |
| * Based on a 2000 calorie diet | | |

Low in sugar

High in niacin

High in selenium

High in vitamin B6

High in zinc

YIELD:

Makes 4 servings

NOTES:

ⓘ If you abstain from alcohol even in cooking, you can substitute a 100% pure grape juice (ensure there is no apple juice in it) and one tsp of distilled vinegar to approximate the same flavor and properties while cooking.

Use a digital meat thermometer to test for doneness:

RARE:             120° degrees F (49° degrees C).

MEDIUM-RARE:    125° degrees F (52° degrees C).

MEDIUM:           130° degrees F (54° degrees C).

## CHERRY-RED FILET MIGNON

Garlic, cherries, and black pepper make a wonderful sauce for this beautiful cut of meat. Serve it with simple sides – some steamed asparagus and a nice pilaf – for a beautiful meal.

### INGREDIENTS:

4 Filet Mignon steaks about 4 to 5 ounces each cut $^3/_4$ inch to 1 inch thick (Beef Tenderloin)

$^1/_2$ lbs fresh Bing cherries, rinsed

$^1/_2$ cup Cabernet or any good dry red wine ① (see NOTES for substitute)

2 cloves garlic, minced

2 TBS extra virgin olive oil

3 TBS balsamic vinegar

4 whole cloves

8 whole peppercorns

1 bay leaf, torn into small pieces

$^1/_2$ tsp freshly ground black pepper

$^1/_2$ tsp salt (Kosher or sea salt is best)

(optional) 1 to 2 tsp honey (pure, raw, local honey is always best)

### SUPPLIES:

10-12 inch cast iron skillet          Sharp knife/cutting board

Saucepan                              Spoon/tongs

### PREPARATION:

Let your steaks fully reach room temperature and dry them completely with paper towels or clean kitchen towel.

If roast-searing, with 10 to 12 inch diameter cast iron skillet inside, set the oven to broil, or bring to about 500° degrees F (260° degrees C).

DIRECTIONS:

Lightly coat steaks with extra virgin olive oil. Rub minced garlic evenly over the steak (press in with your hands); set aside until ready to cook.

Do not salt your steaks just before cooking. Salt brings moisture (water) to the surface of the steak, and the water sits on the surface as you cook the steak. Thus, you are again basically steaming the steak. I know that some people do salt their steaks before cooking, but trust me and don't salt - the result will be juicy, delicious steaks to serve your family and guests! Salt after the steak is cooked to your liking, has rested the required time, and just before serving.

In a large saucepan over medium-high heat, bring the wine and balsamic vinegar to a boil. Tie the cloves, peppercorns, and bay leaf in a bundle with a small piece of cheese cloth. Add the spice bundle to the wine mixture; continue boiling approximately 15 minutes or until mixture is reduced to $1/2$ cup.

While the wine mixture is reducing, pit the cherries. Cut the cherries into quarters and add to the wine mixture. Cover and cook approximately 10 minutes or until the cherries are tender. Season with salt and pepper. Add the sugar to balance the flavors, if needed. Remove the spice bundle from the sauce and discard. Reduce heat to low to keep Cherry-Red Wine Sauce warm until steak are cooked.

There are two methods you can employ to cook these steaks:

1) THE PAN-SEAR TECHNIQUE:

In a cast iron frying pan over medium-high heat, heat 2 TBS extra virgin olive oil just until shimmering, not smoking.

If you like, lightly coat the steaks with extra virgin olive oil and preferred seasonings.

Sear the steaks, moving them with tongs a little so they don't stick to the bottom, approximately 2 to 3 minutes per side turning twice. Cook steak to your desired doneness. Check for doneness with an electronic thermometer (See NOTES).

2) THE ROAST-SEAR TECHNIQUE:

A very hot oven produces a juicy interior. Preheat oven on broil, about 500 degrees F. If you like, lightly coat the steaks with extra virgin olive oil and preferred seasonings.

Place a 10- to 12-inch ovenproof skillet or cast-iron skillet in oven. When oven reaches desired temperature, remove skillet from oven and place on range over high heat. Be extremely careful – the skillet handle will be extremely hot.

Immediately place steaks in the middle of hot, dry pan. If cooking more than one piece of meat, add the steaks carefully so that they do not touch each other. Sear the steaks, cooking 30 seconds to 1 minute without moving. Turn with tongs and cook another 30 seconds to 1 minute turning them just this once.

Now place the cast iron skillet with the steaks inside into the center of the hot oven. Cook an additional 3 to 5 minutes, depending on thickness of steaks and degree of doneness you prefer. Cook to your desired doneness. Check for doneness with an electronic thermometer (See NOTES).

WHEN SUFFICIENTLY COOKED:

Using either of the above methods, When the steaks are crusty-charred and done to your liking, remove from heat entirely and place on a clean, cool dish such as a casserole dish, to catch any juices. Cover loosely with aluminum foil, and let rest at least 5 to 10 minutes before serving.

During this time the meat will continue to cook. The meat temperature will rise anywhere from 5 to 10 degrees after it is removed from the heat and the juices will redistribute. Before moving your steak to a serving platter, add the juices that accumulated from the resting steaks to the Cherry-Red Wine Sauce.

Serve whole or slice thin and fan onto individual serving plates.

Pour the Cherry-Red Wine Sauce over your perfectly cooked steaks just before serving.

YIELD:

Makes 4 servings

NUTRITION:

# Nutrition Facts

Serving Size 104 g

Amount Per Serving

| Calories 156 | Calories from Fat 49 |
|---|---|
| | % Daily Value* |
| Total Fat 5.4g | 8% |
| Saturated Fat 1.5g | 8% |
| Trans Fat 0.0g | |
| Cholesterol 31mg | 10% |
| Sodium 130mg | 5% |
| Total Carbohydrates 7.3g | 2% |
| Sugars 1.1g | |
| Protein 13.4g | |

| Vitamin A 1% | • | Vitamin C 1% |
|---|---|---|
| Calcium 2% | • | Iron 6% |
| * Based on a 2000 calorie diet | | |

Low in sugar

High in niacin

High in selenium

High in vitamin B6

High in zinc

NOTES:

Use a digital meat thermometer to test for doneness:

RARE:               120° degrees F (49° degrees C).

MEDIUM-RARE:   125° degrees F (52° degrees C).

MEDIUM:           130° degrees F (54° degrees C).

ⓘ If you abstain from alcohol even in cooking, you can substitute a 100% pure grape juice (ensure there is no apple juice in it) and one tsp of distilled vinegar to approximate the same flavor and properties while cooking.

## WHOLE RIB EYE

This is an impressive way to serve an excellent cut of beef. Cook this rib eye on your grill. Whether you're hosting a camp full of cowboys, or a patio full of friends, mouths are going to water when you slice into this roast.

INGREDIENTS:

14 to 15 pound single whole rib eye, lip on

4 tablespoons freshly ground black pepper

Brisket Rub (see below)

## BRISKET RUB

$^1/_4$ cup Montreal Steak seasoning mix

2 tbsp freshly ground black pepper

1 tsp dried parsley

1 tbsp chili powder

1 tsp oregano

(optional) 1 tsp sugar or honey (pure, raw, local honey is always best)

SUPPLIES:

Large cast-iron skillet

Measuring cups/spoons

Small bowl

Grill tongs

PREPARATION:

Combine all BRISKET RUB ingredients thoroughly to create the mix.

Heat your grill.

YIELD:

10 to 15 servings

### DIRECTIONS:

In a cast iron skillet large enough to hold the rib eye, place it fat side down. Coat generously with Brisket Rub and freshly ground black pepper. Roll meat and coat fat side. Pat rub and pepper onto the ends.

NOTE: You can optionally lightly coat the rib eye with honey prior to applying the rub. This will help ensure that the Brisket Rub will adhere to the roast. Additionally, you can pan or roast sear the rib eye before placing over the open coals.

Place skillet over medium-hot coals about 30 to 32 inches above the coals. Using clean gloves or thick cloth, turn rib eye once or twice, never cooking it very long with fat side down.

NOTE: When cooking several Whole Rib Eyes, you may use a large fork, but only pierce the fatty lip with the fork. Never pierce the meat.

Allow 4 hours for medium rare and 4 $1/2$ hours for medium. Cook steak to your desired doneness. Check for doneness with an electronic thermometer (See NOTES).

When meat has reached desired temperature, take off coals and let rest 10 minutes.

Cut lip off before serving. Slice into 3/4-inch slices and serve.

### NUTRITION:

# Nutrition Facts

Serving Size 102 g

| Amount Per Serving | |
|---|---|
| Calories 314 | Calories from Fat 215 |
| | % Daily Value* |
| Total Fat 23.9g | 37% |
| Saturated Fat 9.5g | 48% |
| Cholesterol 83mg | 28% |
| Sodium 67mg | 3% |
| Total Carbohydrates 0.9g | 0% |
| Protein 25.2g | |
| Vitamin A 4% • | Vitamin C 1% |
| Calcium 1% • | Iron 14% |
| * Based on a 2000 calorie diet | |

High in protein

Low in sodium

Very low in sugar

NOTES:

Use a digital meat thermometer to test for doneness:

RARE:                    120° degrees F (49° degrees C).

MEDIUM-RARE:     125° degrees F (52° degrees C).

MEDIUM:              130° degrees F (54° degrees C).

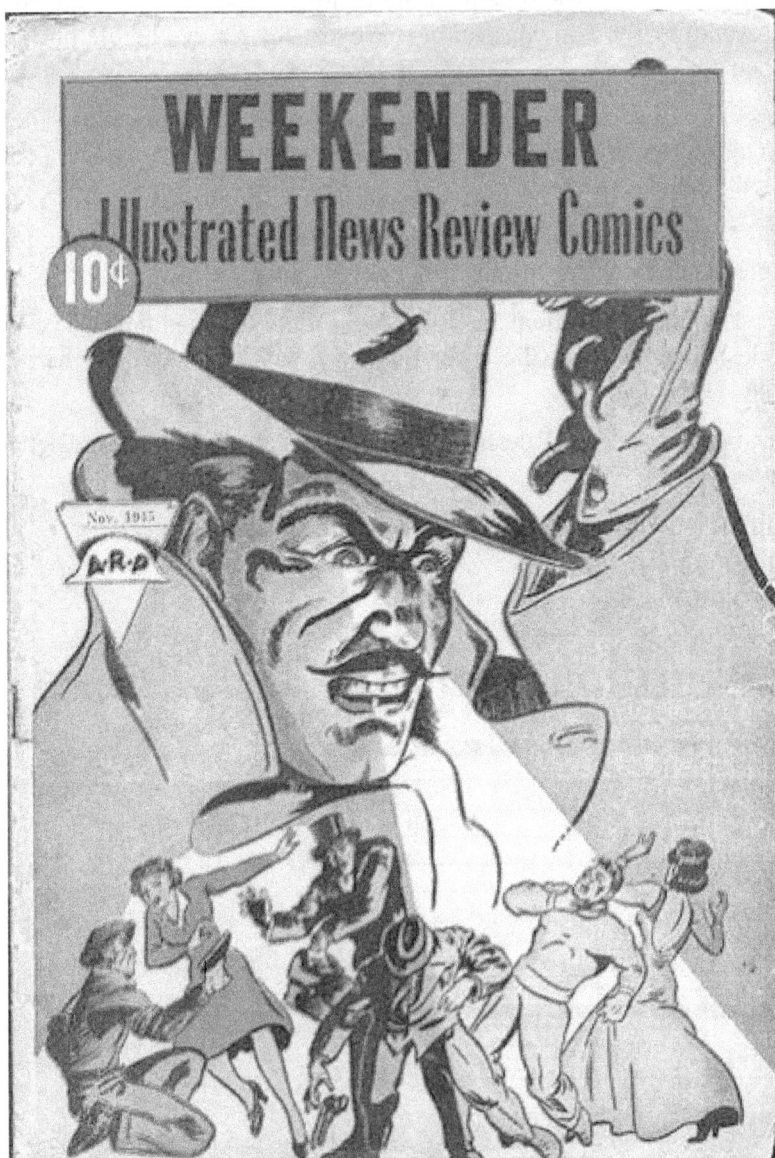

# TEX MEX GROUND BEEF SKILLET   ✳ ⏱ 🌐 🍽

Chili-Mac is one of my kids' favorite dinners. I love how this is served over cornbread instead of sloppy-joe style over hamburger buns. This is a very-quick, easy to make meal – especially if you're using leftover cornbread. I used grass-fed beef, and even with organic vegetables it's still less than $4 per serving.

## INGREDIENTS:

1 lbs lean grass-fed ground beef

4 large slices of Hallee's Old-Fashioned Cornbread ⓘ

1 medium onion, diced ⓘ

1 green bell pepper, diced ⓘ

2 medium ripe (or single 15-ounce can) tomatoes, diced

4 servings freshly prepared (or single 15-ounce can) black beans

1 medium to large avocado, peeled and sliced ⓘ

2 TBS chili powder

plain 0% no-fat yogurt or sour cream for garnish (optional)

## SUPPLIES:

skillet                                          measuring cups/spoons

sharp knife and cutting board         wooden spoon

## PREPARATION:

Prepare Hallee's Old-Fashioned Cornbread.

Drain and rinse black beans.

Slice, twist, pit, scoop, and slice avocado. ⓘ

Dice onion and green pepper.

## YIELD:

4 servings

## DIRECTIONS:

In a skillet over medium-high heat, brown the beef with the onion, green pepper, and chili powder.

Add the diced tomatoes and black beans. Heat thoroughly.

Ladle over squares of cornbread. Top with sliced avocado and yogurt.

## NUTRITION:

| Nutrition Facts | |
|---|---|
| Serving Size 98 g | |
| **Amount Per Serving** | |
| Calories 175 | Calories from Fat 44 |
| | % Daily Value |
| Total Fat 4.9g | 8% |
| Saturated Fat 1.4g | 7% |
| Cholesterol 21mg | 7% |
| Sodium 143mg | 6% |
| Total Carbohydrates 22.6g | 8% |
| Dietary Fiber 4.2g | 17% |
| Sugars 1.5g | |
| Protein 10.1g | |
| Vitamin A 9% • | Vitamin C 22% |
| Calcium 8% • | Iron 13% |
| Based on a 2000 calorie diet | |

Low in sugar

High in vitamin C

Very high in vitamin B6

## NOTES:

For a video demonstrating a quick way to get an avocado to obey your will, check out my 2 minute video here:

http://www.halleethehomemaker.com/2010/12/slice-it-twist-it-pit-it-scoop-it/

ⓘ For information about a tip for chopping vegetables, follow this link:

http://www.halleethehomemaker.com/chopping-veg

# LEMON & OREGANO LAMB CHOPS   ❋ ⏱ 🗡 🍴 🌐 🍲

Juicy lamb chops take a Middle Eastern flair with a quick herb-and-lemon rub and a tangy cucumber-tahini sauce that add a healthy and exotic flavor to this dish. Serve with couscous or rice pilaf and a green salad.

INGREDIENTS:

8 lamb loin chops (1 $\frac{1}{2}$ to 1 $\frac{3}{4}$ lbs total), trimmed

2 lemons

1 TBS chopped fresh oregano (or 1 tsp dried)

$\frac{1}{4}$ cup tahini ① (See NOTES)

$\frac{1}{4}$ cup nonfat plain yogurt, preferably Greek-style

$\frac{1}{4}$ cup diced seeded cucumber, peeled if desired

2 clove garlic, minced

1 TBS chopped fresh parsley

1 TBS filtered water

2 tsp extra virgin olive oil

1 $\frac{1}{4}$ tsp salt, divided (Kosher or sea salt is best)

freshly ground pepper to taste

SUPPLIES:

Large skillet

Juice zester and juicer

Sharp knife/cutting board

Measuring cups/spoons

PREPARATION:

Preheat oven to 400° degrees F (205° degrees C).

Zest the lemons.

Juice the lemons. Save $\frac{1}{4}$ cup for this recipe.

Mince the garlic.

Chop the oregano and the parsley.

Prepare the tahini, if making it yourself.

Peel, seed, and chop the cucumber.

Small bowl and medium bowl

Whisk, mixing spoons

## DIRECTIONS:

Combine lemon zest, oregano, 3/4 teaspoon salt, and pepper in a small bowl. Rub the mixture onto both sides of lamb chops and set aside for at least 10 minutes or refrigerate for up to 1 hour.

Meanwhile, combine tahini, yogurt, cucumber, lemon juice, garlic, parsley, and the remaining 1/2 teaspoon salt in a small bowl. Whisk in enough water to thin the sauce to desired consistency.

Heat oil in a large skillet over medium-high heat. Add the lamb chops and cook until browned on one side, about 2 minutes. Turn them over and transfer the pan to the oven. Roast until an instant-read thermometer inserted horizontally into a chop registers 135 degrees F for medium-rare, 8 to 14 minutes, depending on thickness. Serve the chops with the tahini sauce.

## NUTRITION:

| Nutrition Facts | |
|---|---|
| Serving Size 276 g | |
| **Amount Per Serving** | |
| Calories 505 | Calories from Fat 228 |
| | % Daily Value* |
| Total Fat 25.4g | 39% |
| Saturated Fat 6.9g | 34% |
| Trans Fat 0.0g | |
| Cholesterol 180mg | 60% |
| Sodium 909mg | 38% |
| Total Carbohydrates 8.5g | 3% |
| Dietary Fiber 2.8g | 11% |
| Sugars 2.0g | |
| Protein 59.7g | |
| Vitamin A 4% • | Vitamin C 30% |
| Calcium 15% • | Iron 38% |
| Nutrition Grade B+ | |
| * Based on a 2000 calorie diet | |

Low in sugar
High in niacin
High in phosphorus
Very high in selenium
High in vitamin B12
High in zinc

**YIELD:**

4 servings (2 lamb chops and 3 tablespoons sauce each)

**NOTES:**

ⓘ Tahini is a thick paste of ground sesame seeds. Look for it in large supermarkets in the Middle Eastern section or near other nut butters or find a Middle Eastern market near you. Try to choose brands with no additives or preservatives and always try to use organic if you can – or better yet, make your own. For my recipes for traditional and sunflower substitute tahini, follow these links:

Tasty Traditional Tahini Paste
http://www.halleethehomemaker.com/my-tahini

Savvy Savings Sunflower Seed Substitute Tahini Paste
http://www.halleethehomemaker.com/sunflower-tahini

# Poultry!

In this chapter, you are going to find recipes for roasting a whole chicken to using ground turkey, and so many delicious and wonderful dishes in between.

## SELECTING POULTRY

When selecting poultry, here are a few things to keep in mind:

(1) Try to always purchase free range birds from reputable farms that have humane practices with their fowl. You will pay more per pound for your meat, but at least you know it wasn't raised in unsanitary conditions so crowded it can't even move around.

(2) Try to purchase vegetarian fed birds. Among other things, in the case of chickens at least, this means that it wasn't fed dead chickens. If it's free range, it likely also ate bugs and such, but its feed would have been vegetarian.

(3) Try to purchase local fowl. This will ensure the freshest meat available.

(4) The color of the skin of chicken, duck, and turkey varies from white to yellow. This doesn't mean anything about the freshness or quality of the meat.

## HANDLING POULTRY

When handling poultry, here are some things to keep in mind:

(1) Never defrost frozen meat at room temperature. Always defrost either in the refrigerator or in a pan of cold water (changing the water every 30 minutes).

(2) Never reuse an implement (plate, knife, cutting board, etc.) that has come in contact with raw meat. Always wash with hot, soapy water before reusing.

(3) Wash your hands constantly when handling raw poultry.

(4) Always, <u>always,</u> cook poultry until an instant-read thermometer inserted into the thickest part of the meat registers 165° degrees F (75° degrees C). This is important. ***Even if*** the thermometer reads the proper degree, if the juices are pink, continue cooking. The juices must run clear before the meat is safe to eat.

## PURCHASING POULTRY

The amount of poultry you need to buy varies on what you're buying:

- Whole chicken will feed 1 to 2 people per pound.

- Bone in skin on parts will feed 2 to 3 people per pound

- Boneless, skinless breasts will feed 3 to 4 people per pound

## HOW TO BREAK DOWN A CHICKEN

When I buy chicken, I'll buy a few packages of breasts (on the bone with the skin on), a few packages of wings (whole wings – I break down my own "Buffalo" style), leg-thigh quarters, and the rest that I purchase are whole chickens. It's so much cheaper to break your own chicken down than to pay the price for a "whole cut up chicken". Substantially cheaper. Cheaper like half as much per pound cheaper.

It's very – very – easy to break down a chicken, and the more you do it, the easier it gets. Here's how:

Have a large cutting board, a cleared off area, and a sharp knife.

Lift up a wing to reveal the "underarm" of the bird.

Run your knife all around the joint of the wing.

Once you've cut the skin and meat from around the joint, grab the wing firmly in one hand and the bird in the other and bend the wing backward until the joint pops out.

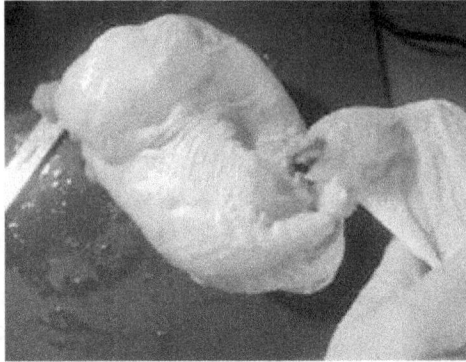

Cut away any remaining skin or meat and the wing is now off of the body.

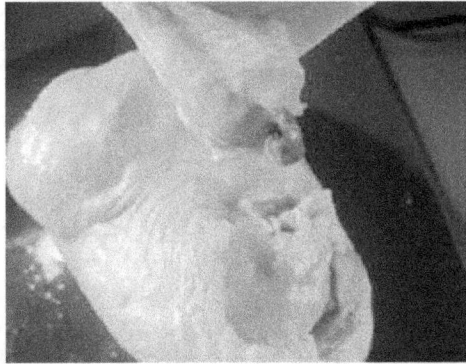

Repeat with the other wing. Lay the chicken breast up. Pull the leg away from the body so that the skin stretches taut.

Take your knife and slice through the skin (you should not be slicing meat – it should only be skin here) until you reach the leg joint.

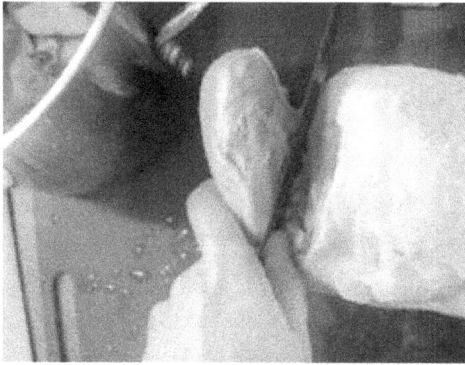

Grip the leg in one hand and the body in the other and bend the leg back until the joint pops out.

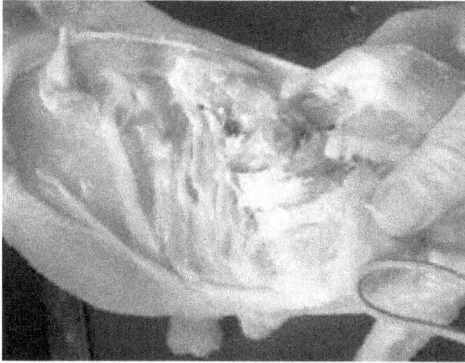

Place the knife between the joint and the bone and cut to remove the leg and the thigh.

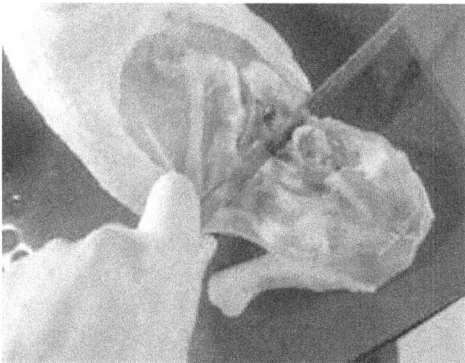

Repeat with the other leg.

What's left are the breasts and back. Place the bird breast up.

There is a breastbone in between the two breasts.
Put your knife against that bone, as close as you can get to it. There is breast meat on it, so the closer you get to that bone, the less meat you lose off of your breast.

Cut down until your breasts separate in half. You can see that bone on the piece my hand is touching, and you can see the meat on the other piece. That is what we just cut – what we just separated.

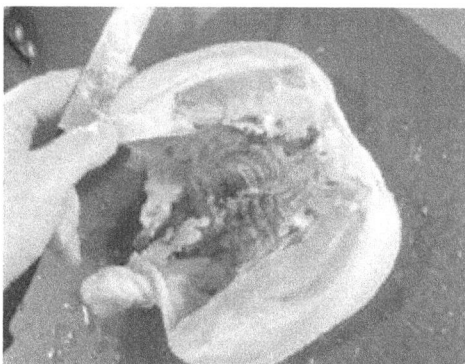

Cut around the bone to remove the breast. (You're cutting around the backbone – I keep the breasts on the bone if I'm going to bake or boil them.)

Repeat with the other breast.

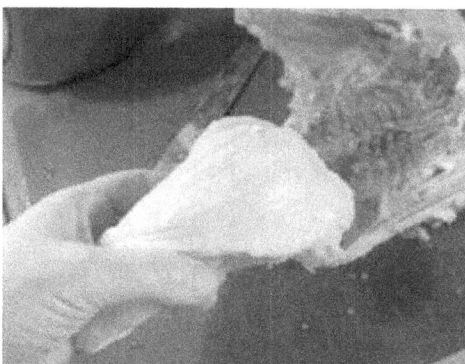

What you have left is the backbone and carcass. Don't discard it. Use this to make a fantastic homemade chicken broth.

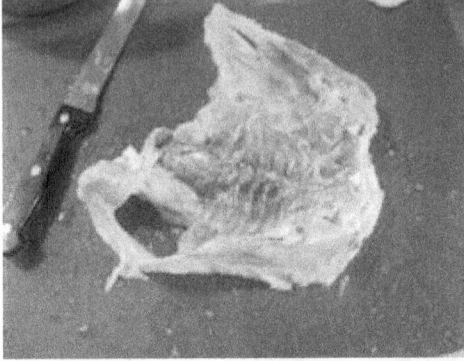

Here is a whole cutup chicken in the pot waiting for its transformation into something delicious! If I hadn't stopped to take pictures, I would have had it done in less than 5 minutes.

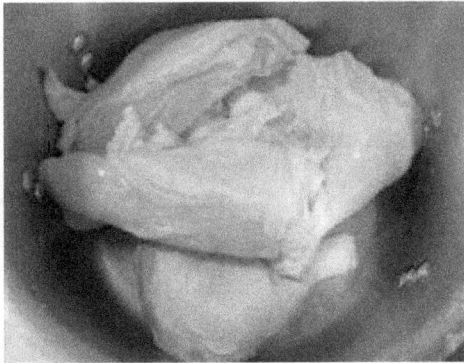

NOTES:

Wipe your area up with paper towels that you discard, then sprinkle the entire area – cutting board, under the cutting board, the countertop, etc. – with baking soda. Let it sit for several minutes before you clean it with your regular cleaner. This will disinfect the area. Do not use the knife, cutting board, or countertop again until you have effectively disinfected it.

ⓘ For the latest information about the current Agricultural Marketing Service USDA standards for grading meat and other consumable commodities, visit the official website at:
http://www.ams.usda.gov/AMSv1.0/Grading

ⓘ I have included the recipe to make Stocky Bird Broth in this cookbook.

## COUNTRY STYLE CHICKEN & RADISH SKILLET DINNER

✺ ⏱ ✡ ❉ 🍽

Radishes used to be part of a family meal, but lately seem to be relegated to just add color in green salads. This is such a quick dinner that is a different blend of tastes than the "norm" and utilizes radishes to their fullest extent. If you're looking for something new to try, seeking out a new family favorite, you found it here.

INGREDIENTS:

1 lbs boned and skinned chicken breasts — cut into thin slices

1 $^1/_2$ cups sliced radishes (single 6-ounce bag)

$^1/_2$ cup Homemade Crock Pot Stocky Bird Broth ⓘ

3 TBS extra virgin olive oil, divided

1 TBS cornstarch

1 TBS soy sauce (Tamari or fermented soy sauce strongly preferred)

$^1/_2$ tsp ground ginger

2 tsp minced garlic

2 cups (about 4 ounces) cut snow peas — cut into $^1/_2$-inch pieces

$^1/_4$ cup sliced green onions (scallions)

SUPPLIES:

Large skillet

Measuring cups/spoons

Mixing bowls

Good sharp knife

Clean cutting board for meat

Clean cutting board for vegetables

PREPARATION:

Cut chicken into bit sized pieces.

Slice radish, onion, and snow peas.

Mince (or finely chop) garlic.

If serving over rice, you will need to prepare the rice. ⓘ

## DIRECTIONS:

In a small bowl, combine broth (OR water), cornstarch, soy sauce and ginger until smooth; set aside.

In a large skillet, heat 2 tablespoons of the oil over high heat until hot. Add chicken and garlic; cook, stirring constantly, just until chicken is cooked through, about 3 minutes. Remove from skillet; set aside.

Add remaining 1 tablespoon oil; heat until hot. Stir in radishes, snow peas and green onions; cook and stir for 1 minute; remove from heat.

Return chicken to skillet. Stir broth mixture; pour into skillet and bring to a boil.

Boil and stir until sauce is clear and slightly thickened, about 1 minute.

Serve over hot cooked rice, if desired.

NUTRITION:

## Nutrition Facts

Serving Size 95 g

Amount Per Serving

| Calories 136 | Calories from Fat 69 |
|---|---|
| | % Daily Value* |
| Total Fat 7.6g | 12% |
| Saturated Fat 1.5g | 8% |
| Trans Fat 0.0g | |
| Cholesterol 40mg | 13% |
| Sodium 186mg | 8% |
| Total Carbohydrates 2.7g | 1% |
| Dietary Fiber 0.7g | 3% |
| Sugars 0.9g | |
| Protein 13.9g | |
| Vitamin A 3% • | Vitamin C 14% |
| Calcium 2% • | Iron 5% |
| * Based on a 2000 calorie diet | |

Low in sugar

High in niacin

High in selenium

High in vitamin C

YIELD:

4 Servings

NOTES:

ⓘ Next time you have chicken or turkey, you can follow the instructions in the Hallee's Homemade Crock Pot Stocky Bird Broth recipe in this cookbook or on my website to make a fabulous and rich broth that will keep for a good long while, especially if you store it using my unconventional Perfect Solution for Freezing Broth. For more information, visit these links:
http://www.halleethehomemaker.com/2009/11/tasty-turkey-broth/

http://www.halleethehomemaker.com/2010/05/the-perfect-solution-for-freezing-broth/

ⓘ For information about a tip for preparing perfect brown rice, follow this link:
http://www.halleethehomemaker.com/2009/11/perfect-brown-rice/

TIP: Cooking in cast iron increases the iron content in food. The longer the food is in contact with the skillet, the more it absorbs.

## QUICK COQ AU VIN

❋ ⏱ ✡ 🍬 🌐 🍷 🍽

Coq au Vin is a red wine-braised chicken-and-vegetable stew that has amazing flavor combinations. Serve with herbed mashed potatoes and green beans for the perfect comfort meal.

### INGREDIENTS:

2 boneless chicken breasts (about 12 ounces each), skin removed, trimmed

$^1/_4$ cup flour (I use fresh ground soft white wheat)

$^1/_2$ cup dry red wine ⓘ (see NOTES for substitute), preferably Zinfandel

$^1/_4$ cup filtered water

1 $^3/_4$ cup (16 oz) Hallee's Heavenly Homemade Bird Broth ⓘ

1 TBS tomato paste

2 TBS extra virgin olive oil, divided

4 ounces baby bella mushrooms

2 large carrots

1 small onion

1 tsp crumbled dried rosemary

2 TBS chopped fresh parsley

$^1/_4$ tsp salt (Kosher or sea salt is best), divided

$^1/_2$ tsp freshly ground black pepper, divided

### SUPPLIES:

Sharp knife/cutting board

Shallow dish

Measuring cups/spoons

Large skillet

Wooden spoon

Small bowl/small whisk

Large plate

Meat thermometer

### PREPARATION:

Cut each chicken breast in half on the diagonal to get 4 portions about equal in weight. (Two will be smaller but thicker, the other two larger but thinner.)

Quarter the mushrooms.

Thinly slice the carrots and onion

Chop the parsley

### DIRECTIONS:

Place flour in a shallow dish. Sprinkle the chicken with $\frac{1}{4}$ teaspoon each salt and pepper and dredge in the flour.

Whisk water with 2 tablespoons of the leftover flour in a small bowl; set aside.

Heat 1 tablespoon oil in a large skillet over medium-high heat. Reduce heat to medium and add the chicken.

Cook, turning once or twice, until lightly browned on all sides, 5 to 7 minutes total. Transfer to a plate.

Add the remaining 1 tablespoon oil to the pan; reduce heat to medium-low.

Add mushrooms, carrots, onion, and rosemary and cook, stirring occasionally, until the vegetables are softened and browned in spots, about 5 minutes.

Add broth, wine, tomato paste, and the remaining $\frac{1}{4}$ teaspoon each salt and pepper. Stir until the tomato paste is dissolved. Bring to a simmer.

Return the chicken and any accumulated juice to the pan. Cover, reduce the heat to maintain a simmer, and cook, stirring once or twice, until an instant-read thermometer inserted into the thickest part of the breast registers 165° degrees F (75° degrees C), 15 to 20 minutes

Transfer the chicken to a serving plate.

Increase the heat under the sauce to medium-high. Stir the water-flour mixture, add it to the pan, and cook, stirring, until the sauce is thickened, about 1 minute. Serve the chicken with the sauce, sprinkled with parsley.

## YIELD:

4 servings; $^1/_2$ breast and $^3/_4$ cup sauce each

## NUTRITION:

# Nutrition Facts

Serving Size 338 g

| Amount Per Serving | |
|---|---|
| **Calories** 326 | Calories from Fat 128 |
| | % Daily Value* |
| **Total Fat** 14.2g | 22% |
| Saturated Fat 2.9g | 15% |
| *Trans* Fat 0.0g | |
| **Cholesterol** 76mg | 25% |
| **Sodium** 588mg | 25% |
| **Total Carbohydrates** 14.9g | 5% |
| Dietary Fiber 2.4g | 10% |
| Sugars 4.0g | |
| **Protein** 29.0g | |
| Vitamin A 12% • | Vitamin C 16% |
| Calcium 3% • | Iron 16% |

High in niacin
High in selenium
Very high in vitamin B6

## NOTES:

ⓘ If you abstain from alcohol even in cooking, you can substitute a 100% pure grape juice (ensure there is no apple juice in it) and one tsp of distilled vinegar to approximate the same flavor and properties while cooking.

ⓘ I have included a recipe for Hallee's Heavenly Homemade Bird Broth in this cookbook. If you don't have stock on hand, be sure to use a good organic stock with low or no salt.

# SKILLET SHEPHERD'S PIE

Traditionally, shepherd's pie is made in an oven. This skillet recipe made with chicken instead of the traditional lamb is as good as anything you can pull out of the oven - a delicious combination of meat, potatoes, and vegetables. Serve with a salad and a loaf of crusty French bread for a whole meal.

INGREDIENTS:

2 chicken breasts, bone in, skin on

$1/2$ tsp salt (Kosher or sea salt is best)

$1/2$ tsp fresh ground black pepper

$1\ 1/3$ cup Hallee's Homemade Cream of Mushroom Soup ⓘ

$1/2$ cup whole milk

16 oz package frozen mixed vegetables, thawed and drained

4 cup hot Wonderful Whipped Potatoes

$1/4$ tsp onion powder

$1/4$ tsp fresh ground black pepper

SUPPLIES:

| | |
|---|---|
| Large skillet | Measuring cups/spoons |
| Cutting board | Baking sheet |
| Sharp knife | Strainer |

PREPARATION:

Preheat oven to 425° degrees F (220° degrees C). Sprinkle chicken with $1/2$ tsp salt and $1/2$ tsp fresh ground pepper. Place in oven and bake for 20-25 minutes or until an instant-read thermometer inserted into the thickest part of the breast registers 165° degrees F (75° degrees C). Remove from oven and let cool. Remove meat from the bone and skin and cut into cubes cube.

Prepare mashed potatoes.

Prepare cream of mushroom soup.

Rinse and drain vegetables.

## DIRECTIONS:

In a large skillet, combine all the ingredients except the potatoes over high heat. Mix well.

Cook 5 to 8 minutes, or until heated through, stirring frequently.

Remove from the heat and dollop with the potatoes. Serve immediately.

## YIELD:

Serves 4

## NUTRITION:

### Nutrition Facts

Serving Size 542 g

| Amount Per Serving | |
|---|---|
| Calories 462 | Calories from Fat 107 |
| | % Daily Value* |
| Total Fat 11.8g | 18% |
| Saturated Fat 3.8g | 19% |
| Cholesterol 73mg | 24% |
| Sodium 1482mg | 62% |
| Total Carbohydrates 58.3g | 19% |
| Dietary Fiber 5.1g | 20% |
| Sugars 5.8g | |
| Protein 31.6g | |
| Vitamin A 101% • | Vitamin C 8% |
| Calcium 13% • | Iron 20% |

High in niacin
Very high in vitamin A
High in vitamin B6

## NOTES:

ⓘ I have also included a recipe for Hallee's Homemade Cream of Mushroom Soup in this cookbook. If you don't have it on hand and have no time to whip up a batch, be sure to use a good organic soup with low or no salt. If you would like to make your own batch, follow this link:
http://www.halleethehomemaker.com/cream-of-mushroom

ⓘ For information about a tip for preparing the perfect batch of mashed potatoes, follow this link:
http://www.halleethehomemaker.com/whipped-potatoes

## PEACH GLAZED CHICKEN ⏱ 🚫 🍽

This recipe was adapted from a Georgia-style barbecued chicken with peach sauce. Traditionally, chicken is slow roasted in a pit of coals. This recipe is done simply in a skillet over a hot stove. The end result is a perfectly delightful combination of sweet and savory, and a nice face-lift to the standard baked chicken fare.

**INGREDIENTS:**

$^1/_4$ cup flour (I use fresh ground soft white wheat)

4 chicken breast halves (1 to 1 $^1/_2$ lbs), boneless and skinless

2 TBS unsalted butter

2 $^1/_2$ cup peaches, sliced (20 oz frozen package, thawed)

1 $^1/_2$ cup light brown sugar, firmly packed

2 celery stalks

1 small onion

$^1/_2$ red bell pepper

2 TBS lemon juice

$3/_4$ tsp cayenne pepper

$^1/_2$ tsp salt (Kosher or sea salt is best)

**SUPPLIES:**

Shallow dish

Measuring cups/spoons

Large skillet

Sharp knife/cutting board

Platter for holding chicken

**PREPARATION:**

Chop ① Chop celery, onion, and bell pepper.

Peel and slice peaches, if using fresh.

## DIRECTIONS:

Place flour in a shallow dish. Dip chicken breasts in flour, coating completely. In a large skillet, melt butter over medium-high heat. Add coated chicken and brown 2 to 3 minutes per side.

Transfer chicken to a platter and set aside.

Add remaining ingredients to skillet and cook 4 to 5 minutes, until sauce begins to thicken.

Return chicken to skillet and cook 8 to 10 minutes, or until no pink remains in chicken and sauce has thickened.

To enjoy every last bit of the peach sauce, serve this over hot cooked rice.

## YIELD:

Serves 4

## NUTRITION:

| Nutrition Facts | | |
|---|---|---|
| Serving Size 430 g | | |
| **Amount Per Serving** | | |
| Calories 634 | Calories from Fat 112 | |
| | | % Daily Value* |
| Total Fat 12.5g | | 19% |
| Saturated Fat 3.8g | | 19% |
| Trans Fat 0.0g | | |
| Cholesterol 161mg | | 54% |
| Sodium 552mg | | 23% |
| Total Carbohydrates 75.4g | | 25% |
| Dietary Fiber 4.0g | | 16% |
| Sugars 66.4g | | |
| Protein 57.6g | | |
| Vitamin A 26% | • | Vitamin C 58% |
| Calcium 9% | • | Iron 19% |
| Nutrition Grade B+ | | |
| * Based on a 2000 calorie diet | | |

Very high in niacin
High in selenium
Very high in vitamin B6
High in vitamin B12

## NOTES:

ⓘ For information about a tip for chopping vegetables, follow this link: http://www.halleethehomemaker.com/chopping-veg

## PAN-ROASTED CHICKEN & GRAVY ❄ ⏱ 🎄 ⚸ 🍽

There is hardly anything better than roasted chicken and gravy. It is one of my go-to meals, and a family favorite. A cast-iron skillet is the perfect vessel for a simple roast chicken, and making the gravy in the same pan in which you cook the chicken makes some of the best gravy possible.. Almost every side dish, be it vegetables, legumes, pasta or rice, goes well with it.

### INGREDIENTS:

3 ¹/₂ lbs chicken, giblets removed

1 ¹/₂ cup Hallee's Heavenly Homemade Bird Broth ⓘ

1 ¹/₂ tsp fresh thyme leaves

1 tsp organic grapeseed oil

2 tsp unsalted butter, softened, divided

2 tsp flour (I use fresh ground soft white wheat)

1 clove garlic, minced

¹/₂ tsp salt (Kosher or sea salt is best)

¹/₄ tsp freshly ground white pepper

1 TBS minced fresh flat-leaf parsley, for garnish

### SUPPLIES:

| | |
|---|---|
| Large skillet | Sharp knife |
| Small bowl/spoon | Cutting board |
| Whisk | Measuring cups/spoons |

### PREPARATION:

Preheat oven to 400° degrees F (190° degrees C).

Mince the garlic.

Chop the parsley.

Chop the thyme.

## DIRECTIONS:

Mash garlic and salt into a paste in a small bowl, using the back of a spoon. Stir in pepper and thyme. With a sharp knife, remove any excess fat from chicken. Dry the inside with a paper towel. With your fingers, loosen the skin over the breasts and thighs to make pockets, being careful not to tear the skin. Rub the garlic mixture over the breast and thigh meat.

Heat oil and 1 teaspoon butter in a 12-inch cast-iron skillet over medium heat. Add the chicken and cook, turning often, until nicely browned on all sides, about 10 minutes.

Transfer the pan to the oven and roast the chicken until the internal temperature in the thickest part of the thigh reaches registers 165° degrees F (75° degrees C) - 50 minutes to 1 hour. Transfer the chicken to a clean cutting board; tent with foil.

Meanwhile, mash the remaining 1 teaspoon butter and flour in a small bowl until a paste forms. Place the pan (use caution, the handle will be hot) over medium-high heat. Add broth and bring to a simmer, stirring to scrape up any browned bits. Gradually whisk in the butter-flour paste a few bits at a time, until the gravy thickens, about 8 minutes. Remove from the heat and let stand for 5 minutes, allowing any fat to rise to the top. Skim off the fat with a spoon.

Carve the chicken and serve with the gravy. Garnish with parsley, if desired.

## NUTRITION:

| Nutrition Facts | |
|---|---|
| Serving Size 346 g | |
| **Amount Per Serving** | |
| Calories 549 | Calories from Fat 212 |
| | % Daily Value* |
| Total Fat 23.6g | 36% |
| Saturated Fat 6.7g | 33% |
| Trans Fat 0.0g | |
| Cholesterol 239mg | 80% |
| Sodium 622mg | 26% |
| Total Carbohydrates 1.3g | 0% |
| Protein 77.9g | |
| Vitamin A 5% • | Vitamin C 2% |
| Calcium 5% • | Iron 21% |
| Nutrition Grade B- | |
| * Based on a 2000 calorie diet | |

Very low in sugar
Very high in niacin
High in selenium
High in vitamin B6

YIELD:

Serves 6

NOTES:

ⓘ I have included a recipe for Hallee's Heavenly Homemade Bird Broth in this cookbook. If you don't have stock on hand, be sure to use a good organic stock with low or no salt.

## SOUTHERN FRIED CHICKEN  ❄ ⏱ 🔥 🌾 🍲

Southern style fried chicken is one of my family's favorite meals. I use the guidelines found in the front of this book and break up a whole chicken and fry that. This batter is crispy and packed full of flavor. If you use a good oil (like grapeseed oil), you'll have a clean, crunchy shell and a moist and wonderful interior.

**INGREDIENTS:**

3 ¹/₂ lbs chicken

buttermilk (enough to cover cut up chicken - about 3-4 cups)

Flour, for dredging (I use soft white wheat)

Grapeseed oil for frying

spice mix as follows (I made a quadruple recipe then put it in a shaker – like a Parmesan cheese shaker at pizza place):

> 2 tablespoons kosher salt
>
> 2 tablespoons Hungarian paprika
>
> 2 teaspoons garlic powder
>
> 1 teaspoon cayenne pepper

**SUPPLIES:**

Skillet (cast iron works best)

Large bowl to soak chicken in buttermilk

Bowl to dredge chicken in flour (I think a pie plate is easiest)

Sturdy tongs

cooling rack and paper towels on which to drain chicken

**PREPARATION:**

Soak the chicken in buttermilk. 8 hours is ideal. I've done it for 20 minutes in a rush. Just try to soak it as long as you can.

Make the spice mix.

Heat the oil to 325° degrees F (160° degrees C).

**DIRECTIONS:**

Drain the buttermilk from the chicken. Liberally sprinkle both sides with spice mix. Dredge in flour.

Cook the chicken in the oil (when the chicken is in the pan, there should be just enough oil to come up halfway up the chicken) for 10-12 minutes on each side, or until the internal temperature reaches 180° degrees F (80° degrees C).

Place on cooling racks over paper towels to drain.

If you'd like to make gravy, using the drippings in the pan:

Pour all but a tablespoon of the oil out of the pan, leaving the drippings. With a whisk, blend in 1-2 tablespoons of flour, until a thick paste is formed. Continuing to stir with the whisk, and over medium heat, add 1 cup of milk per tablespoon of flour. Stir with whisk until it thickens and boils. Boil 1 minute. Salt and pepper to taste.

NUTRITION:

## Nutrition Facts

Serving Size 179 g

**Amount Per Serving**

**Calories** 279 | Calories from Fat 54

| | % **Daily Value**[*] |
|---|---|
| **Total Fat** 6.0g | **9**% |
| Saturated Fat 1.5g | **8**% |
| **Cholesterol** 106mg | **35**% |
| **Sodium** 1236mg | **51**% |
| **Total Carbohydrates** 12.0g | **4**% |
| Dietary Fiber 1.0g | **4**% |
| Sugars 1.5g | |
| **Protein** 41.9g | |

| | |
|---|---|
| Vitamin A 17% | Vitamin C 2% |
| Calcium 5% | Iron 12% |

**Nutrition Grade B**

* Based on a 2000 calorie diet

Very low in sugar
Very high in niacin
High in selenium
High in vitamin B6

YIELD:

Serves 6

NOTES:

Remove chicken breasts from bone before frying to make more room in the pan and cut down on their cooking time. Everything else is cooked on the bone.

> One of the most wonderful things about cast iron skillets and other all-metal cookware is that you can transfer your dish from the grill to the stove top or from the stove top to the oven or from the oven back to the stove top.

## SWEET & SOUR CHICKEN WITH VEGETABLES

This skillet recipe has amazing Asian flavors, and some beautiful fruit & vegetables. Serve over rice and you have an entire meal.

INGREDIENTS:

2 $^1/_2$ lbs chicken thighs, boneless, skinless, cut into thin strips

2 TBS extra virgin olive oil (or organic grapeseed oil or rice oil for a lighter flavor)

1 $^1/_4$ cup fresh pineapple chunks (or 20 oz can, drained)

$^1/_2$ cup water chestnuts (8 oz can, drained), sliced

1 cup fresh broccoli florets

1 cup fresh snow peas

1 medium-sized red bell pepper

2 TBS soy sauce (Tamari or fermented soy sauce strongly preferred)

2 TBS cornstarch

1 TBS honey (pure, raw, local honey is always best)

1 TBS Hallee's Homemade Organic Ketchup ⓘ

1 TBS white vinegar

SUPPLIES:

Sharp knife/cutting board (one for meat, one for veggies)

Measuring cups/spoons

Large skillet

Whisk

PREPARATION:

Slice the chicken into thin strips

Break down the pineapple and slice into small chunks.

Cut the broccoli and the bell pepper into bite-sized pieces.

Trim the snow peas.

## DIRECTIONS:

In a large cast iron skillet, heat oil over medium-high heat. Add chicken and stir-fry for 4 to 5 minutes, or until no pink remains.

Add pineapple chunks, water chestnuts, broccoli, and red pepper. Stir-fry for 3 to 4 minutes, or until the vegetables are crisp-tender.

In a small bowl, combine the reserved pineapple liquid, the soy sauce, vinegar, ketchup, cornstarch, and sugar; mix well with a whisk. Stir into skillet and cook 3 minutes. Add snow peas and cook 1 minute, or until sauce has thickened. Serve immediately.

## YIELD:

Serves 6

## NUTRITION:

| Nutrition Facts | |
|---|---|
| Serving Size 344 g | |
| **Amount Per Serving** | |
| Calories 523 | Calories from Fat 172 |
| | % Daily Value* |
| Total Fat 19.1g | 29% |
| Saturated Fat 4.6g | 23% |
| Trans Fat 0.0g | |
| Cholesterol 168mg | 56% |
| Sodium 504mg | 21% |
| Total Carbohydrates 28.1g | 9% |
| Dietary Fiber 2.1g | 8% |
| Sugars 9.1g | |
| Protein 57.6g | |
| Vitamin A 23% • | Vitamin C 130% |
| Calcium 7% • | Iron 21% |
| Nutrition Grade A- | |
| * Based on a 2000 calorie diet | |

High in niacin
High in selenium
High in vitamin B6
Very high in vitamin C

## NOTES:

This recipe cooks up just as well in your wok.

ⓘ I have included a recipe for Hallee's Homemade Organic Ketchup in this cookbook. If you don't have your own homemade ketchup on hand, be sure to use a good organic brand with low or no salt.

PRIZE PINEAPPLE CHICKEN TENDERS

## PINEAPPLE CHICKEN TENDERS ❄ ⏱ ✡ 🍬 🚫 🌐 🎞

This dish has a nice flavor with the pineapple and sweet peppers. It's a fun dish with lots of colors and is wonderful served over rice.

**INGREDIENTS:**

$^1/_2$ cup plus 2 tsp (divided) Hallee's Sherry-Ginger Asian Sauce ①

1 lbs boneless, skinless chicken tenders

1 cup pineapple

1 TBS pineapple juice

1 TBS organic grapeseed oil

$^1/_2$ red bell pepper

$^1/_2$ yellow bell pepper

$^1/_2$ green bell pepper

$^1/_4$ cup green onions

**SUPPLIES:**

Large skillet

resealable bag

Measuring cups/spoons

Sharp knife/cutting board

**PREPARATION:**

Prepare sauce.

Slice the peppers and onions

If using fresh pineapple, cut the pineapple into chunks and juice pineapple to make 1 TBS

**DIRECTIONS:**

In a large resealable bag, combine chicken and Hallee's Sherry-Ginger Asian Sauce. Marinate for 15 to 20 minutes.

Heat oil in skillet over medium-high heat. Add the chicken and cook for 6 to 8 minutes or until chicken is no longer pink in center. Remove chicken to a plate and cover with foil to keep warm.

Add the peppers to the skillet and cook 4 to 5 minutes or until crisp tender.

Add green onions, pineapple, 1 tablespoon pineapple juice, and 2 teaspoons marinade to skillet, cook and stir for about 1 minute.

Spoon onions and pineapple over warm chicken tenders.

YIELD:

Serves 4

NUTRITION:

## Nutrition Facts

Serving Size 165 g

Amount Per Serving

| Calories 195 | Calories from Fat 73 |
| --- | --- |
| | % Daily Value* |
| Total Fat 8.1g | 13% |
| Saturated Fat 1.9g | 10% |
| Trans Fat 0.0g | |
| Cholesterol 67mg | 22% |
| Sodium 92mg | 4% |
| Total Carbohydrates 7.1g | 2% |
| Dietary Fiber 1.1g | 5% |
| Sugars 5.2g | |
| Protein 22.5g | |
| Vitamin A 21% • | Vitamin C 87% |
| Calcium 2% • | Iron 7% |

Nutrition Grade A-
* Based on a 2000 calorie diet

Low in sodium
High in manganese
High in niacin
High in selenium
High in vitamin A
High in vitamin B6
Very high in vitamin C

NOTES:

This recipe cooks up just as well in your wok.

ⓘ I included a recipe for Hallee's Sherry-Ginger Asian Sauce in this cookbook. If you don't make your own, choose a good organic option with low or no salt and no chemicals or MSG.

When storing cast iron cookware, always store with the lids off or with the lids ajar. This will help keep moisture from building up and causing rust. In damp environments, consider tossing a dry paper towel or two inside cast iron sauce pans, skillets, or Dutch Ovens to help absorb excess humidity.

## LEMON CHICKEN WITH SNOW PEAS

Lemon chicken is one of my daughter's favorite dishes. This original recipe called for boneless, skinless breasts, but I love it made with bone-in, skin-on chicken thighs. The meat has so much flavor, and it is delicious with the sauce.

INGREDIENTS:

4 chicken thighs, bone-in, skin-on

10 oz snow peas

2 eggs

$^1/_4$ cup grated Parmesan cheese

$^1/_4$ cup parsley (plus more for garnish), chopped

$^1/_2$ cup Hallee's Heavenly Homemade Bird Broth ⓘ

$^1/_4$ cup fresh lemon juice (about 2 lemons)

$^1/_2$ tsp salt (Kosher or sea salt is best)

$^1/_4$ tsp fresh ground black pepper

$^1/_4$ cup flour (I use fresh ground soft white wheat)

2 garlic cloves, chopped

2 TBS extra virgin olive oil

3 TBS unsalted butter

1 lemon, cut into wedges

SUPPLIES:

Large skillet

Sharp knife/cutting board

Small bowl/Whisk

Cheese grater

Juicer

Tongs

Small dish for dredging the chicken

PREPARATION:

Grate the Parmesan cheese

Juice 2 of the 3 lemons

Cut one lemon into wedges

Chop the garlic

Chop the parsley

**DIRECTIONS:**

In a large bowl, lightly beat eggs. Add Parmesan cheese, $^{1}/_{4}$ cup parsley, $^{1}/_{4}$ cup broth, 2 TBS lemon juice, salt, and pepper. Coat chicken in flour, then dip into egg mixture. Set aside.

In a large skillet, sauté garlic in extra virgin olive oil over medium for 30 seconds. Add chicken and cook until an instant-read thermometer inserted into the thickest part of the thigh registers 165° degrees F (75° degrees C), about 7 minutes each side. Remove to a plate.

In same skillet, melt butter. Stir in $^{1}/_{4}$ cup broth and 2 TBS lemon juice. Bring to a boil; cook 30 seconds. Pour over chicken; serve with snow peas. Garnish with lemon and parsley.

**NUTRITION:**

# Nutrition Facts

Serving Size 345 g

Amount Per Serving

| Calories 563 | Calories from Fat 291 |
|---|---|
| | % Daily Value* |
| Total Fat 32.4g | 50% |
| Saturated Fat 12.4g | 62% |
| Trans Fat 0.0g | |
| Cholesterol 245mg | 82% |
| Sodium 744mg | 31% |
| Total Carbohydrates 13.7g | 5% |
| Dietary Fiber 3.5g | 14% |
| Sugars 3.9g | |
| Protein 54.1g | |
| Vitamin A 32% • | Vitamin C 90% |
| Calcium 21% • | Iron 24% |

Nutrition Grade B
* Based on a 2000 calorie diet

Low in sugar
High in niacin
High in phosphorus
High in selenium
High in vitamin C

**YIELD:**

Serves 4.

**NOTES:**

ⓘ I have included a recipe for Hallee's Heavenly Homemade Bird Broth in this cookbook. If you don't have stock on hand, be sure to use a good organic stock with low or no salt.

## MUSHROOM LOVER'S CHICKEN ❄ ⏱ 🍷 🍽

This dish takes chicken and pairs it with a mushroom sauce that is savory and delightful. Serve it with herbed potatoes for a beautiful company-worthy dish

**INGREDIENTS:**

4 chicken breast halves

$^1/_2$ cup flour (I use fresh ground soft white wheat)

1 cup Hallee's Heavenly Homemade Bird Broth ⓘ

$^1/_2$ cup dry white wine ⓘ (see NOTES for substitute), optional

2 TBS extra virgin olive oil

3 TBS unsalted butter

1 small onion

$^1/_2$ lbs (8 oz) fresh white mushrooms, sliced

$^1/_4$ tsp salt (Kosher or sea salt is best)

$^1/_8$ tsp fresh ground black pepper

**SUPPLIES:**

Large skillet

Sharp knife/cutting board

Measuring cups/spoons

Small dish for dredging chicken

Plate

Whisk

Tongs

**PREPARATION:**

Chop the onion ⓘ

Slice the mushrooms

**DIRECTIONS:**

In a shallow dish, combine flour, salt, and pepper; mix well. Dip chicken in flour mixture, coating well.

In a large skillet, heat oil over medium-high heat. Add chicken and cook 4 to 5 minutes per side, or until golden. Remove chicken to a plate and cover.

Melt butter in the same skillet. Add onions and mushrooms; saute 5 to 7 minutes, stirring occasionally. Stir in chicken broth and wine and bring to a boil then reduce heat to low. Return chicken to skillet and cook 6 to 8 more minutes, or until no pink remains, turning chicken once.

Spoon mushroom sauce over chicken and serve immediately.

YIELD:

Serves 4

NUTRITION:

| Nutrition Facts | | |
| --- | --- | --- |
| Serving Size 343 g | | |
| Amount Per Serving | | |
| Calories 519 | Calories from Fat 245 | |
| | | % Daily Value* |
| Total Fat 27.2g | | 42% |
| Saturated Fat 9.6g | | 48% |
| Cholesterol 153mg | | 51% |
| Sodium 530mg | | 22% |
| Total Carbohydrates 15.5g | | 5% |
| Dietary Fiber 2.8g | | 11% |
| Sugars 2.2g | | |
| Protein 47.5g | | |
| Vitamin A 7% | • | Vitamin C 7% |
| Calcium 3% | • | Iron 24% |

Low in sugar
High in niacin
High in selenium
Very high in vitamin B6

NOTES:

ⓘ If you prefer not to use wine, simple substitute it with an additional ½ cup chicken broth. If you abstain from alcohol even in cooking, you can substitute a 100% pure grape juice (ensure there is no apple juice in it) and one tsp of distilled vinegar to approximate the same flavor and properties while cooking.

ⓘ I have included a recipe for Hallee's Heavenly Homemade Bird Broth in this cookbook. If you don't have stock on hand, be sure to use a good organic stock with low or no salt.

ⓘ For information about a tip for chopping vegetables, follow this link:

http://www.halleethehomemaker.com/chopping-veg

## TURKEY TACO PIE

❋ ⏱ 🌾 🌐 🍲

Taco pie was one of my favorite dishes growing up. It's fun to have the kick of flavor found in tacos in something else. Kids love helping prepare this meal as well.

### INGREDIENTS:

1 lbs ground turkey breast

2 cups romaine lettuce, shredded

1 large tomato, chopped ①

$^1/_2$ cup (2 ounces) real Cheddar cheese, shredded

2 cups Hallee's Homemade Refried Beans ① (or 16 oz gluten-free vegetarian canned)

1 cup Hallee's Homemade Spicy Salsa ①, (see NOTES)

1 tsp ground cumin

extra virgin olive oil or unsalted butter according to personal taste

### SUPPLIES:

Sharp knife/cutting board

Large skillet

Wooden spoon

Cheese grater

### PREPARATION:

Shred the lettuce

Dice the tomatoes

Shred the cheese

### DIRECTIONS:

Lightly grease the inside of the skillet with either extra virgin olive oil or unsalted butter according to personal taste.

Heat over medium-high heat. Add the turkey breast and ground cumin, and cook for 5 to 6 minutes, or until the turkey is no longer pink, stirring to break up the turkey.

Stir in the refried beans and salsa; bring to a boil.

Reduce the heat to low; simmer for 5 minutes, or until well combined and heated through, stirring frequently. Remove the skillet from the heat, scrape down the sides with a spatula, and spread the mixture evenly in the skillet.

Arrange the lettuce, tomato, and Cheddar cheese in concentric circles on top of the turkey mixture; serve immediately.

**NUTRITION:**

## Nutrition Facts

Serving Size 406 g

| Amount Per Serving | |
|---|---|
| Calories 479 | Calories from Fat 178 |
| | % Daily Value* |
| Total Fat 19.7g | 30% |
| Saturated Fat 9.0g | 45% |
| Trans Fat 0.0g | |
| Cholesterol 124mg | 41% |
| Sodium 1020mg | 43% |
| Total Carbohydrates 26.8g | 9% |
| Dietary Fiber 8.7g | 35% |
| Sugars 4.1g | |
| Protein 48.3g | |
| Vitamin A 20% | Vitamin C 26% |
| Calcium 30% | Iron 30% |
| Nutrition Grade B | |
| * Based on a 2000 calorie diet | |

Low in sugar
High in phosphorus
High in selenium

**YIELD:**

Serves 6

**NOTES:**

Top with sour cream or plain yogurt and guacamole. Serve with organic corn chips.

ⓘ Look for prepared fresh salsa in the supermarket refrigerator section near other dips and spreads. Try to choose brands with no additives or preservatives and always try to use organic if you can or make your own. For my recipe for homemade spicy salsa, follow this link:
http://www.halleethehomemaker.com/homemade-salsa

ⓘ To make this a gluten-free recipe, use seasoning with no added starch from a gluten-containing source, gluten-free vegetarian refried beans. For my recipe for homemade Homemade Refried Beans, follow this link:
http://www.halleethehomemaker.com/my-refried-beans

ⓘ For information about a tip for chopping vegetables, follow this link:
http://www.halleethehomemaker.com/chopping-veg

## CHICKEN & PEPPER TRIP

This is such a perfect dish for a luncheon menu or a different take on a dinner. The marinade can be made well in advance and refrigerated for weeks. It is simply an Italian dressing, and leftovers can be used to dress a salad.

INGREDIENTS:

### FOR THE ENTRÉE:

4 chicken breasts, bone-in, skin-on

1 TBS extra virgin olive oil

2 green bell peppers

2 red bell peppers

2 yellow bell peppers

$1/2$ tsp garlic powder

$1/4$ tsp fresh ground black pepper

10 oz fresh spinach, washed and trimmed

3 TBS shredded Parmesan cheese (optional)

### FOR THE MARINADE:

1/2 cup apple cider or white wine vinegar

2/3 cup extra virgin olive oil

1 tablespoons of water

1 1/2 tsp dried oregano

1 1/2 tsp salt (Kosher or sea salt is best)

3/4 tsp garlic powder

3/4 tsp onion powder

3/4 tsp honey (local, raw honey preferred)

3/4 tsp dried parsley

$1/4$ tsp ground black pepper

$1/4$ tsp dried basil

pinch dried thyme

**SUPPLIES:**

Jar with lid or small bowl with whisk

Large bowl with lid

Sharp knife/cutting board

Large skillet

Tongs

**PREPARATION:**

MAKE MARINADE:

Mix all ingredients in a jar, put the lid on, and shake it up. -OR- mix in small bowl with a whisk until mixed.

Wash and trim spinach.

Cut peppers into strips.

Shred Parmesan cheese.

**YIELD:**

Serves 6

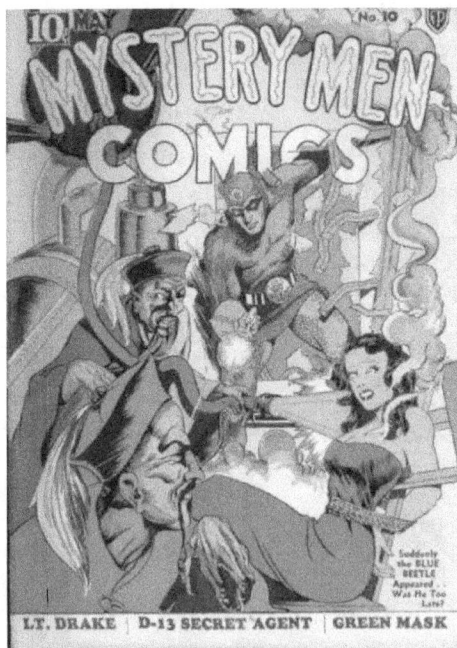

## DIRECTIONS:

Pour 3/4 cup of marinade. Add chicken and mix well. Cover and refrigerate for 1 hour.

Heat a large skillet over medium-high heat until hot. Add 1 Tablespoon olive oil.

Place chicken in pan, discarding marinade, and cook or 7 to 8 minutes per side, or until until an instant-read thermometer inserted into the thickest part of the breast registers 165° degrees F (75° degrees C).

Remove chicken from pan and cut chicken off of the bone; set aside.

Add peppers, garlic powder, and black pepper to pan and cook 4 to 5 minutes, or until crisp-tender, stirring occasionally.

Return de-boned chicken to pan and cook until heated through.

Place spinach in a large bowl and add chicken mixture, and remaining $^1/_4$ cup marinade; toss well. Sprinkle with Parmesan cheese.

Top with chicken and peppers. Serve immediately.

## NUTRITION:

# Nutrition Facts

Serving Size 341 g

| Amount Per Serving | |
|---|---|
| Calories 459 | Calories from Fat 299 |
| | % Daily Value* |
| Total Fat 33.2g | 51% |
| Saturated Fat 6.2g | 31% |
| Trans Fat 0.0g | |
| Cholesterol 90mg | 30% |
| Sodium 776mg | 32% |
| Total Carbohydrates 9.7g | 3% |
| Dietary Fiber 3.3g | 13% |
| Sugars 4.9g | |
| Protein 32.2g | |
| Vitamin A 97% • | Vitamin C 201% |
| Calcium 13% • | Iron 19% |
| Nutrition Grade B | |
| * Based on a 2000 calorie diet | |

High in niacin
Very high in vitamin A
Very high in vitamin C

## NOTES:

You can serve this with seasoned, buttered pasta for a delicious Italian flavored dish.

## TURKEY SAUSAGE PASTA SAUCE  ❄ ✝ ✡ ℘ 🌐 🍽

Turkey Italian sausage is my go-to meat for making pasta sauce. This sauce is light and fresh - made with fresh basil and sweet peppers. It's delicious served over a whole grain pasta and topped with fresh grated Parmesan cheese.

### INGREDIENTS:

1 lbs turkey Italian sausage

1 lbs whole grain angel hair pasta

1 $^3/_4$ cup (28 oz can, undrained) diced tomatoes with juice

2 TBS chopped fresh basil

1 yellow bell pepper

2 garlic cloves, minced

1 TBS extra virgin olive oil

filtered water as needed

$^1/_2$ tsp salt (Kosher or sea salt is best)

$^1/_4$ tsp fresh ground black pepper

### SUPPLIES:

Large skillet

Sharp knife/cutting board

Measuring cups/spoons

Stock pot for preparing pasta

Colander

Wooden spoon

### PREPARATION:

Dice peppers ①

Mince garlic

Prepare pasta according to package directions. Drain.

Remove sausage from casings.

⚬ DIRECTIONS:

In a large skillet, heat oil over medium heat. Add sausage, bell pepper, and garlic and cook until meat is browned, breaking up meat with wooden spoon as it cooks. Stir in tomatoes, salt, and pepper, and simmer 10 to 15 minutes.

Stir the basil into the sauce and serve over the pasta.

⚬ NUTRITION:

| Nutrition Facts | |
|---|---|
| Serving Size 77 g | |
| **Amount Per Serving** | |
| Calories 179 | Calories from Fat 90 |
| | % Daily Value* |
| Total Fat 10.0g | 15% |
| Saturated Fat 2.6g | 13% |
| Cholesterol 77mg | 26% |
| Sodium 372mg | 15% |
| Total Carbohydrates 0.2g | 0% |
| Protein 20.7g | |
| Vitamin A 1% • | Vitamin C 0% |
| Calcium 2% • | Iron 9% |

High in Vitamin C

⚬ YIELD:

Serves 4

⚬ NOTES:

ⓘ For information about a tip for chopping vegetables, follow this link:
http://www.halleethehomemaker.com/chopping-veg

## TANDA JUNGLE PRINCESS APPLE & GINGER CHICKEN STIR FRY

# APPLE & GINGER CHICKEN STIR FRY ❄ ✡ 🍬 🌿 🌐 🍽

Such a delicious dish. Take apples, ginger, soy – they all come together to flavor the chicken in a beautiful way. Serve over rice for an amazing dinner.

### INGREDIENTS:

4 chicken breasts, bone-in, skin-on

2 medium apples

2 tsp sesame oil

4 green onions

$^1/_3$ lbs pea pods

1 small sweet red pepper

2 garlic cloves

2 TBS ginger

10 shitake and/or white mushrooms

$^1/_4$ tsp pepper

$^1/_3$ cup unsweetened applesauce

$^1/_3$ cup Hallee's Heavenly Homemade Bird Broth ⓘ

2 TBS apple cider vinegar

2 TBS soy sauce

1 TBS cornstarch

### SUPPLIES:

| | |
|---|---|
| Large skillet | Sharp knife |
| Measuring cups/spoons | Cutting board |
| Wooden spoon | Small bowl/whisk |

### PREPARATION:

| | |
|---|---|
| Core and slice apples | Cut the pepper into strips |
| Slice green onions | Mince the garlic and ginger |

## DIRECTIONS:

Heat sesame oil in nonstick skillet or wok. Add garlic and ginger, and stir for approximately 30 seconds. Add chicken and cook for 7 to 8 minutes per side, or until an instant-read thermometer inserted into the thickest part of the breast registers 165° degrees F (75° degrees C).

Remove chicken from pan and cut chicken off of the bone; set aside.

Add vegetables to skillet and cook while stirring until tender crisp, sprinkle with ground pepper.

In a small bowl, whisk together applesauce, soy sauce, vinegar, cornstarch and chicken broth or water.

Add chicken to vegetables, add sauce mixture and cook until sauce is thickened and clear. Add apples during last five minutes of preparation. Serve over steamed brown rice.

## NUTRITION:

### Nutrition Facts

Serving Size 429 g

| Amount Per Serving | |
|---|---|
| Calories 422 | Calories from Fat 122 |
| | % Daily Value* |
| Total Fat 13.5g | 21% |
| Saturated Fat 3.4g | 17% |
| Trans Fat 0.0g | |
| Cholesterol 130mg | 43% |
| Sodium 648mg | 27% |
| Total Carbohydrates 27.7g | 9% |
| Dietary Fiber 6.5g | 26% |
| Sugars 15.2g | |
| Protein 45.8g | |
| Vitamin A 26% • | Vitamin C 90% |
| Calcium 7% • | Iron 20% |
| Nutrition Grade A- | |
| * Based on a 2000 calorie diet | |

High in niacin
High in selenium
High in vitamin B6
Very high in vitamin C

## YIELD:

Serves 4.

## NOTES:

ⓘ I have included a recipe for Hallee's Heavenly Homemade Bird Broth in this cookbook. If you don't have stock on hand, be sure to use a good organic stock with low or no salt.

## TURKEY BREAKFAST SAUSAGE

Even though we don't eat pork, I love sausage. But, reading the label of the brand of turkey sausage that I used to buy, I realized that they used BHA and BHT in their sausage — two preservatives that I try to avoid. So, I started looking at making my own sausage and discovered that it is surprisingly easy to make — all you need is a pound of ground turkey and some spices that are likely already on hand.

INGREDIENTS:

1 lb. ground turkey

$^3/_4$ tsp salt (Kosher salt is best)

$^1/_2$ tsp ground nutmeg

$^1/_2$ tsp dried sage

$^1/_2$ tsp dried thyme

$^1/_4$ tsp cayenne pepper

SUPPLIES:

skillet

bowl

measuring spoons

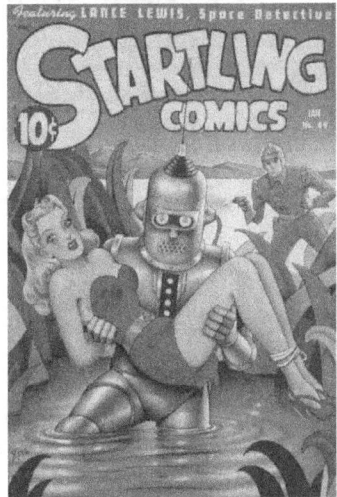

### DIRECTIONS:

Thoroughly mix all ingredients together. I use my hands to make sure it's all completely mixed. Just remember, you're handling raw poultry, so follow careful handling practices and wash your hands with hot water and soap when you're done.

If you want, you can form into patties and freeze. Or, you can form into patties and cook right away. Or, you can crumble into the pan and fry it up to make sausage gravy.

When cooking, because of the low fat content of turkey, I put about a TBS of olive oil in my pan. Then, fry over medium to medium-high heat until the internal temperature of patties reaches at least 165° degrees F (75° degrees C). If you're frying them as crumbles, cook until thoroughly browned.

### NUTRITION:

# Nutrition Facts

Serving Size 77 g

Amount Per Serving

| Calories 179 | Calories from Fat 90 |
|---|---|
| | % Daily Value* |
| Total Fat 10.0g | 15% |
| Saturated Fat 2.6g | 13% |
| Cholesterol 77mg | 26% |
| Sodium 372mg | 15% |
| Total Carbohydrates 0.2g | 0% |
| Protein 20.7g | |

| Vitamin A 1% | • | Vitamin C 0% |
|---|---|---|
| Calcium 2% | • | Iron 9% |

Very low in sugar
Very high in selenium

### YIELD:

Serves 6

### NOTES:

ⓘ For information about a tip for chopping vegetables, follow this link:
http://www.halleethehomemaker.com/chopping-veg

# Meatless Meals!

This section is full of meatless recipes. Some are side items, some are main dishes, and some can be used either way.

My family eats a vegetarian meal most nights during the week, so I'm always on the hunt for new recipes. Even when I do serve meat, with most dinners I serve a vegetable on the side. However, I often grow fatigued of coming up with side dishes that are different from the typical green beans or corn. It is always nice to have some other options, easy to make, on hand.

When cooking vegetables, I always try to start with fresh vegetables. If you can't get fresh, frozen is better than canned. These recipes all start with fresh or frozen. If you use canned, you may need to adjust cooking times or salt amounts.

Another benefit of cooking with cast iron is that it heats food very evenly and allows for precise control of cooking temperatures. When cooking with cast iron, try to always preheat your skillet before placing your food into in. This promotes browning and helps ensure your food cooks evenly.

## BALSAMIC-GLAZED BRUSSELS SPROUTS

Even my 5-year-old likes Brussels sprouts. I serve them all the time. This recipe, with a balsamic glaze, adds an amazing kick of acid for these vegetables, and almost gives them a coleslaw like taste.

**INGREDIENTS:**

1 lbs Brussels sprouts

1 TBS extra virgin olive oil

1 onion

$\frac{1}{4}$ cup balsamic vinegar

**SUPPLIES:**

Sharp knife/cutting board

Skillet

Measuring cups/spoons

Saucepan

**PREPARATION:**

Trim the Brussels sprouts and cut them in half.

Thinly slice the onion.

**DIRECTIONS:**

In a saucepan, bring 2 quarts water to a boil.

Add Brussels sprouts and reduce heat to medium. Cook 10 minutes, or until sprouts are crisp-tender and very green; drain.

In a medium skillet over medium heat, heat oil. Cook onion until tender. Add vinegar and sprouts. Stir to coat sprouts and cook until heated through.

**YIELD:**

Serves: 4

NUTRITION:

## Nutrition Facts

Serving Size 160 g

Amount Per Serving

| Calories 94 | Calories from Fat 35 |
|---|---|
| | % Daily Value* |
| Total Fat 3.9g | 6% |
| Saturated Fat 0.6g | 3% |
| Trans Fat 0.0g | |
| Cholesterol 0mg | 0% |
| Sodium 29mg | 1% |
| Total Carbohydrates 13.0g | 4% |
| Dietary Fiber 4.8g | 19% |
| Sugars 3.7g | |
| Protein 4.1g | |
| Vitamin A 17% • | Vitamin C 166% |
| Calcium 4% • | Iron 8% |

Nutrition Grade A
* Based on a 2000 calorie diet

No cholesterol
Low in sodium
Very high in dietary fiber
High in manganese
High in potassium
High in thiamin
High in vitamin A
Very high in vitamin B6
Very high in vitamin C

NOTES:

ⓘ Just trim the brown off of the stems of the Brussels sprouts. If you trim too close to the globe of the vegetable, it will fall apart - keep part of the stem there to hold it all together.

## VEGETARIAN FAJITAS

These fajitas have such a wonderful flavor explosion in your mouth, that even the most die-hard meat eaters won't miss the meat. It's a wonderful meal to make with ingredients fresh out of a summer garden, and takes just minutes to whip up.

INGREDIENTS:

2 small zucchini, julienned

2 medium small yellow squash, julienned

1 large onion, sliced

1 green bell pepper, cut into thin strips

1 red bell pepper, cut into thin strips

1 (8.75 ounce) can organic whole kernel corn, drained

1 (15 ounce) can organic black beans, drained

$^1/_4$ cup red wine vinegar -OR- apple cider vinegar if fasting

$^1/_4$ cup extra virgin olive oil

2 TBS extra virgin olive oil (reserved)

1 tsp dried oregano

1 tsp chili powder

dash to tsp garlic powder (to taste)

dash fine ground kosher salt OR fine ground sea salt (to taste)

dash fresh ground black pepper (to taste)

OPTIONAL:

1 tsp sugar (fine milled raw organic is best) -OR- 2 tsp honey if fasting

SUPPLIES:

sharp knife/cutting board

heavy skillet

spoons/measuring cups/measuring spoons

Large bowl.

## PREPARATION:

Julienne cut zucchini and small yellow squash.

Slice onion.

Cut pepper into thin strips

## DIRECTIONS:

In a large bowl combine olive oil, vinegar, oregano, chili powder, garlic salt, salt, pepper and sugar. To the marinade add the zucchini, yellow squash, onion, green pepper and red pepper. Marinate vegetables in the refrigerator for at least 30 minutes, but not more than 24 hours.

Heat oil in a large skillet over medium-high heat. Drain the vegetables and saute until tender, about 10 to 15 minutes. Stir in the corn and beans; increase the heat to high for 5 minutes, to brown vegetables.

## YIELD:

6 servings

## NUTRITION:

| Nutrition Facts | |
|---|---|
| Serving Size 333 g | |
| **Amount Per Serving** | |
| Calories 435 | Calories from Fat 133 |
| | % Daily Value* |
| Total Fat 14.8g | 23% |
| Saturated Fat 2.3g | 11% |
| Cholesterol 0mg | 0% |
| Sodium 23mg | 1% |
| Potassium 1628mg | 47% |
| Total Carbohydrates 62.0g | 21% |
| Dietary Fiber 14.9g | 60% |
| Sugars 7.9g | |
| Protein 18.7g | |
| Vitamin A 33% | Vitamin C 132% |
| Calcium 12% | Iron 30% |
| Nutrition Grade A | |
| * Based on a 2000 calorie diet | |

Very high in vitamin C
High in dietary fiber
High in potassium
High in thiamin
Very low in sodium
No cholesterol

## NOTES:

Serve with warm whole wheat tortillas and fresh guacamole.

## SPINACH PASTA & RICE     ✳ ⏱ ✝ 🌿 ✡ 🍲

This is a colorful, handsome dish that can be used as a side-dish or even a main dish. Top it with grated Parmesan cheese for a little bit of a kick.

**INGREDIENTS:**

2 TBS extra virgin olive oil

$\frac{1}{2}$ cup mini ring pasta

1 cup cooked Perfect Brown Rice ⓘ

1 $\frac{1}{4}$ cup (10-ounce frozen package) spinach, chopped

2 $\frac{1}{2}$ cups vegetable broth (or chicken broth)

**SUPPLIES:**

Large skillet

Colander

Cutting board

Sharp knife

Measuring cups/spoons

Wooden spoon

**PREPARATION:**

Thaw spinach and drain. Chop.

**DIRECTIONS:**

In a large skillet, heat oil over medium-high heat.

Add pasta and cook 1 to 2 minutes, or until golden, stirring frequently.

Stir in remaining ingredients and bring to a boil.

Reduce heat to low, cover and simmer 20 to 25 minutes, or until all liquid is absorbed and rice is tender.

**YIELD:**

Serves: 4

NUTRITION:

## Nutrition Facts

Serving Size 284 g

| Amount Per Serving | |
|---|---|
| Calories 302 | Calories from Fat 86 |
| | % Daily Value* |
| Total Fat 9.5g | 15% |
| Saturated Fat 1.6g | 8% |
| Cholesterol 0mg | 0% |
| Sodium 535mg | 22% |
| Total Carbohydrates 45.6g | 15% |
| Dietary Fiber 3.5g | 14% |
| Sugars 0.9g | |
| Protein 9.7g | |

| | | |
|---|---|---|
| Vitamin A 133% | • | Vitamin C 33% |
| Calcium 9% | • | Iron 19% |

Nutrition Grade A
* Based on a 2000 calorie diet

No cholesterol
Low in sugar
Very high in manganese
High in magnesium
Very high in vitamin A
High in vitamin C

NOTES:

Rings, orzo, or any type of miniature pasta can be used - even alphabet pasta for an educational as well as tasty side dish.

ⓘ For information about a tip for preparing perfect brown rice, follow this link:

http://www.halleethehomemaker.com/2009/11/perfect-brown-rice/

## ITALIAN-STYLE ZUCCHINI & TOMATOES

I love the flavor of zucchini with tomatoes, and often in the summertime as zucchini is coming out of the garden, chop some up and toss it into my spaghetti sauce. This recipe keeps the vegetables fresh. The basil and garlic provide the perfect blend of seasonings.

INGREDIENTS:

3 medium zucchini

1 cup filtered water

1 TBS unsalted butter

$^1/_2$ onion, thinly sliced

1 cup ripe grape or cherry tomatoes, cut in half

$^1/_2$ tsp dried basil

$^3/_4$ tsp garlic powder

SUPPLIES:

Sharp knife/cutting board

Skillet

Measuring cups/spoons

PREPARATION:

Slice the zucchini.

Thinly slice the onion.

Cut the tomatoes in half.

DIRECTIONS:

In a large skillet, add zucchini and water; bring to a boil over high heat.

Reduce heat to low and simmer, covered, until zucchini is just tender, about 4 minutes. Drain zucchini.

In same skillet, melt butter over medium heat. Add zucchini, onions, tomatoes, basil, and garlic and simmer about 5 minutes, or until heated through.

**YIELD:**

Serves 6

**NUTRITION:**

# Nutrition Facts

Serving Size 202 g

**Amount Per Serving**

| Calories 63 | Calories from Fat 29 |
|---|---|
| | % Daily Value* |
| Total Fat 3.2g | 5% |
| Saturated Fat 1.9g | 9% |
| Cholesterol 8mg | 3% |
| Sodium 37mg | 2% |
| Total Carbohydrates 8.0g | 3% |
| Dietary Fiber 2.4g | 10% |
| Sugars 4.2g | |
| Protein 2.3g | |

| | | |
|---|---|---|
| Vitamin A 14% | • | Vitamin C 54% |
| Calcium 2% | • | Iron 6% |

Nutrition Grade A
* Based on a 2000 calorie diet

High in dietary fiber
High in manganese
High in magnesium
High in phosphorus
Very high in potassium
High in riboflavin
Very high in vitamin A
Very high in vitamin B6
Very high in vitamin C

**NOTES:**

I use zucchini and yellow summer squash interchangeably - so don't be afraid to mix it up when you make this meal.

## BLACK BEAN QUESADILLAS

Quesadillas are a nice break from the standard lunch fare, and are so much more filling that I would have realized. Pepper Jack cheese and salsa add a little kick to the flavorful beans. I've been known to top quesadillas with plain yogurt and avocados.

### INGREDIENTS:

1 $^3/_4$ cup cooked organic black turtle beans

$^1/_2$ cup shredded Monterey Jack cheese, preferably pepper Jack

$^1/_2$ cup Hallee's Homemade Spicy Salsa ⓘ, divided (see NOTES)

4 (8-inch) Hallee's Homemade Whole-Wheat Flour Tortillas ⓘ, (see NOTES)

2 tsp organic grapeseed oil, divided

1 ripe avocado, diced

### SUPPLIES:

Sharp knife/cutting board

Cheese grater

Large skillet

### PREPARATION:

Prepare the beans. The best way to prepare your beans for this recipe is to soak your beans overnight, drain and rinse, then add $^1/_4$ tsp salt and cook for 2 hours or until done.

Shred the cheese

Dice the avocado

### DIRECTIONS:

Combine beans, cheese, and $^1/_4$ cup salsa in a medium bowl. Place tortillas on a work surface. Spread 1/2 cup filling on half of each tortilla. Fold tortillas in half, pressing gently to flatten.

Heat 1 teaspoon oil in a large skillet over medium heat. Add quesadillas and cook, turning once, until golden on both sides, 2 to 4 minutes total. Transfer to a cutting board and tent with foil to keep warm. Repeat with the remaining 1 teaspoon oil and quesadillas. Serve the quesadillas with avocado and the remaining salsa.

 YIELD:

4 servings

 NUTRITION:

| Nutrition Facts | | |
|---|---|---|
| Serving Size 316 g | | |
| Amount Per Serving | | |
| Calories 394 | Calories from Fat 181 | |
| | | % Daily Value* |
| Total Fat 20.1g | | 31% |
| Saturated Fat 3.3g | | 16% |
| Trans Fat 0.0g | | |
| Cholesterol 1mg | | 0% |
| Sodium 987mg | | 41% |
| Total Carbohydrates 49.0g | | 16% |
| Dietary Fiber 11.2g | | 45% |
| Sugars 4.2g | | |
| Protein 11.8g | | |
| Vitamin A 4% | • | Vitamin C 9% |
| Calcium 6% | • | Iron 11% |

Very low in cholesterol
High in dietary fiber

 NOTES:

ⓘ For my recipe for homemade whole-wheat flour tortillas, follow this link: http://www.halleethehomemaker.com/homemade-flour-tortillas

ⓘ Look for prepared fresh salsa in the supermarket refrigerator section near other dips and spreads. Try to choose brands with no additives or preservatives and always try to use organic if you can or make your own. For my recipe for homemade spicy salsa, follow this link: http://www.halleethehomemaker.com/homemade-salsa

ⓘ For information about a tip for chopping vegetables, follow this link: http://www.halleethehomemaker.com/chopping-veg

## WINTER SQUASH STUFFED WITH WILD RICE

I love finding a recipe that will be my new go-to recipe for entertaining. We had company for dinner, and since we're observing a Daniel Fast, this was our main course using acorn squash. The next evening, we served a soup and had this as a side using pumpkins. The rice is amazing alone, but pared with the winter squash, it is remarkable. This would be beautiful gracing any holiday table.

INGREDIENTS:

6 acorn squashes or 20 mini-pumpkins

2 TBS plus 1 TBS olive oil, divided

2 medium onions

3 stalks celery

$^1/_2$ tsp dried sage

$^1/_2$ tsp salt

2 cups wild rice blend (I used Lundberg Wild Rice Blend ⓘ)

3 cups vegetable stock

$^3/_4$ cup pecans

$^1/_2$ cup dried cherries

1 cup scallion greens

salt and pepper, to taste

SUPPLIES:

sharp knife and cutting board

measuring cups/spoons

medium bowl for soaking rice

strainer

pastry brush

skillet

cookie sheet with parchment paper

oven-proof skillet with lid

**PREPARATION:**

Cover the rice with water and soak for several hours. Drain.

Cut the acorn squash in half and scrape out the seeds and membranes. Or, cut the tops off of the pumpkins and scoop out the seeds and the membranes, reserving the tops. Brush the insides of the squash with 2 TBS olive oil. Cover cookie sheet with parchment paper. Place the squash cut side down on the paper.

Chop the celery and dice the onion. ⓘ

Preheat oven to 425° degrees F (220° degrees C)

**DIRECTIONS:**

In an oven-proof pan, heat the remaining 1 TBS of olive oil over medium-high heat. Cook, stirring regularly, until the vegetables are translucent. Add the salt and the sage. Mix well. Stir in the rice and cook for two or three minutes to toast it.

Add the vegetable stock. Stir and cover with lid.

Place the squash and the rice in preheated 425° degrees F (220° degrees C) oven for 45 minutes or until the liquids have absorbed in the rice and the flesh of the squash is tender. Remove from oven. Let the rice sit for 10 minutes.

While the rice is sitting, heat a small skillet over medium-high heat. Add the pecans and toast about two or three minutes, stirring constantly.

Remove from heat and roughly chop the pecans. Chop the cherries. Slice the scallion greens. Add the pecans, cherries, and scallion greens to the rice. Mix well. Add salt and pepper to taste.

Place the squash in the serving dish. Spoon the rice mixture into the squash. Serve.

YIELD:

about 12 main servings, about 20 side dishes

NUTRITION:

## Nutrition Facts

Serving Size 349 g

Amount Per Serving

| Calories 296 | Calories from Fat 78 |
|---|---|
| | % Daily Value* |
| Total Fat 8.7g | 13% |
| Saturated Fat 1.0g | 5% |
| Trans Fat 0.0g | |
| Cholesterol 0mg | 0% |
| Sodium 137mg | 6% |
| Potassium 842mg | 24% |
| Total Carbohydrates 51.0g | 17% |
| Dietary Fiber 5.5g | 22% |
| Sugars 2.4g | |
| Protein 5.6g | |

| | | |
|---|---|---|
| Vitamin A 18% | • | Vitamin C 47% |
| Calcium 10% | • | Iron 13% |

Nutrition Grade A-
* Based on a 2000 calorie diet

Low in saturated fat
No cholesterol
Low in sodium
Low in sugar
Very high in vitamin B6
High in vitamin C

NOTES:

Any winter squash will work for this recipe.

I am in no way affiliated with Lundburg but thier mix was good and I recommend them. Check out their website:

http://www.lundberg.com/Products/Products_Home.aspx

ⓘ For information about a tip for chopping vegetables, follow this link:

http://www.halleethehomemaker.com/chopping-veg

# VEGETABLE LO MEIN

My husband calls me a "noodle girl". In a restaurant, if the choice is lo mein or rice, I'll always go for the lo mein. This is a nice vegetarian dish that can be served as a side or as a main dish. Don't be afraid to substitute different vegetables and see what other flavors you can come up with!

## INGREDIENTS:

2 TBS extra virgin olive oil

2 TBS toasted sesame oil

1 large garlic clove

1-inch piece of ginger

8 ounces white mushroom caps

4 scallions (including 3 inches of green)

8 oz snow peas

1 carrot

8 oz linguine (preferably whole wheat)

4 TBS soy sauce (Tamari or fermented soy sauce strongly preferred)

1 TBS rice or cider vinegar

## SUPPLIES:

Large skillet

Sharp knife/cutting board

Small saucepan

Large stock pot/colander

Bowl

Vegetable peeler

Measuring cups/spoons

Slotted spoon

Wooden spoon

### PREPARATION:

Thinly slice the garlic.

Peel and thinly slice the ginger

Thinly slice the mushrooms and scallions.

Peel and slice the carrots

Blanch the snow peas and carrots by bringing water to a boil in the saucepan. Add the peas and carrots and cook for 2 minutes.

Remove from the water and immediately plunge into cold water to stop the cooking process.

Cook the pasta according to the package directions

### DIRECTIONS:

Heat the olive and sesame oils in a large skillet over medium-low heat.

Add the garlic and ginger and cook until just golden, stirring occasionally, to flavor the oil, 3 to 4 minutes.

Remove the garlic and ginger from the skillet with a slotted spoon and discard, reserve the oil.

Using the same skillet, saute the mushrooms and scallions over medium heat, stirring, for 2 minutes.

Remove from the heat and add the snow peas and carrot. Toss to combine.

Place the cooked linguine in a large bowl and add the vegetable mixture along with the oil from the skillet.

Add the soy sauce and vinegar and toss well to combine. Taste and adjust seasonings if necessary.

Let rest for at least 2 hours before serving for flavors to brighten. Pack in a plastic container, cover tightly, and refrigerate overnight.

### YIELD:

Makes 6 one-cup servings

NUTRITION:

| Nutrition Facts | |
|---|---|
| Serving Size 253 g | |
| **Amount Per Serving** | |
| Calories 246 | Calories from Fat 91 |
| | % Daily Value* |
| Total Fat 10.1g | 16% |
| Saturated Fat 1.3g | 7% |
| Trans Fat 0.0g | |
| Cholesterol 11mg | 4% |
| Sodium 612mg | 25% |
| Total Carbohydrates 30.7g | 10% |
| Dietary Fiber 3.1g | 12% |
| Sugars 2.4g | |
| Protein 10.5g | |
| Vitamin A 11% • | Vitamin C 38% |
| Calcium 3% • | Iron 10% |
| Nutrition Grade B- | |
| * Based on a 2000 calorie diet | |

Low in cholesterol
High in vitamin B6
High in vitamin C

NOTES:

You can add any vegetables or meat you want to this dish - go with combinations that sound good to you and don't be afraid to experiment!

# PEA & MUSHROOM FRIED RICE ❄ ⏱ ✝ 🌰 ✡ 🔥 🌐 🍽

Fried rice is often a dish I make as the main dish to a meal. My kids love it. They help me and think they're working a grill in a Hibachi restaurant. This dish is wonderful in its simpleness. The rice, soy, and ginger add a really nice flavor to the traditional green peas. Serve this as a side dish or as the star of the meal.

### INGREDIENTS:

3 TBS extra virgin olive oil

1 tsp sesame oil

1 lbs mixed mushrooms, sliced

1 clove garlic, minced

1 TBS grated fresh ginger

6 scallions, sliced thin

$1^1/_2$ cups cooked Perfect Brown Rice ⓘ

$^1/_2$ tsp salt (Kosher or sea salt is best)

$^1/_4$ cup soy sauce (Tamari or fermented soy sauce strongly preferred)

1 cup frozen peas

### SUPPLIES:

Sharp knife/cutting board

Micro plane to grate ginger

Colander to rinse peas

Large skillet

Measuring cups/spoons

Plate

### PREPARATION:

Prepare the rice

Thaw and rinse the peas

Slice mushrooms and the scallions

Mince the garlic

Grate the ginger

### DIRECTIONS:

In a large skillet, heat 2 Tbsp extra virgin olive oil over medium-high heat. Add mushrooms; cook, stirring, 5 minutes. Remove to plate.

Heat remaining olive oil in pan over medium heat; add garlic, ginger, and scallions. Stir for 30 seconds. Increase heat to high; add rice, salt, soy sauce, peas, and reserved mushrooms. Cook, stirring, 2 minutes. Remove from heat; stir in sesame oil.

### YIELD:

Serves 4

### NUTRITION:

| Nutrition Facts | |
|---|---|
| Serving Size 380 g | |
| **Amount Per Serving** | |
| Calories 1,098 | Calories from Fat 170 |
| | % Daily Value* |
| Total Fat 18.9g | 29% |
| Saturated Fat 3.1g | 16% |
| Cholesterol 0mg | 0% |
| Sodium 1233mg | 51% |
| Potassium 862mg | 25% |
| Total Carbohydrates 208.8g | 70% |
| Dietary Fiber 12.0g | 48% |
| Sugars 2.7g | |
| Protein 23.2g | |
| Vitamin A 21% • | Vitamin C 14% |
| Calcium 12% • | Iron 34% |
| Nutrition Grade A | |
| * Based on a 2000 calorie diet | |

Low in saturated fat
No cholesterol
Very low in sugar
Very high in manganese

### NOTES:

ⓘ For information about a tip for preparing perfect brown rice, visit this link: http://www.halleethehomemaker.com/2009/11/perfect-brown-rice/

## POTATO CHIPS

Since potatoes are in the "dirty dozen," I try very hard to just get organic potato chips. But, organic potato chips are SO EXPENSIVE. It doesn't seem worthwhile to even buy that little tiny bag. My 4-year-old son brought me a potato and said, "Can you make me some potato chips?" I love the fact that he deduced that potato chips come from potatoes, and that he was confident I could produce them. Which I did. They were amazing. Our daughter came home from softball practice and ate the leftovers, then asked if I would make them for her the next morning for her lunch. I will never purchase bagged potato chips again.

INGREDIENTS:

potatoes

oil (I used canola oil – please make sure your canola is organic because of GMO's. You can use any kind of oil – grapeseed, safflower, peanut, olive — whatever your frying oil of preference is, use it)

sea salt

SUPPLIES:

mandolin

skillet

slotted spoon

paper towels

PREPARATION:

Wash your potatoes really well. I keep the skin on mine.

Heat your oil to 375° degrees F (190° degrees C).

DIRECTIONS:

Using the mandolin, slice your potatoes really thin. My thinnest setting is 1/8 inch. I'm sure there are people out there with the knife skills to do this without a mandolin – I'm not one of them.

Gently slide the sliced potatoes into the oil, one slice at a time.

The oil is going to immediately bubble all around the slice. As it cooks, it's going to curl up and start to crisp.

Once it curls up, try to turn it over (some don't make it over – that's fine) and keep cooking until they start to brown.

Remove them from the oil and place on a paper towel. I immediately sprinkle them with sea salt.

Try to keep the kids from eating them all before they all get cooked.

### YIELD:

Serves: 4

### NUTRITION:

| Nutrition Facts | |
|---|---|
| Serving Size 395 g | |
| **Amount Per Serving** | |
| Calories 281 | Calories from Fat 24 |
| | % Daily Value* |
| Total Fat 2.7g | 4% |
| Trans Fat 0.0g | |
| Cholesterol 0mg | 0% |
| Sodium 23mg | 1% |
| Total Carbohydrates 59.4g | 20% |
| Dietary Fiber 9.1g | 36% |
| Sugars 4.3g | |
| Protein 6.3g | |
| Vitamin A 1% • | Vitamin C 124% |
| Calcium 3% • | Iron 11% |
| Nutrition Grade A | |
| * Based on a 2000 calorie diet | |

Very low in saturated fat
No cholesterol
Very low in sodium
High in dietary fiber
High in potassium
High in vitamin B6
Very high in vitamin C

### NOTES:

ⓘ Store leftovers in a sealed container.

## CRISPY POTATOES WITH EGGS & GREEN BEANS

This is the perfect meal to accompany a brunch. Or, add a side salad and you have a nice dinner for two.

INGREDIENTS:

2 lbs potatoes

4 large eggs

1 cup fresh or frozen green beans, cut into 1-inch pieces

2 TBS extra-virgin olive oil

2 clove garlic, minced

$1/_8$ tsp crushed red pepper

$1/_2$ tsp salt (Kosher or sea salt is best)

$1/_2$ tsp freshly ground black pepper

paprika (optional)

SUPPLIES:

Sharp knife/cutting board

Saucepan to cook fresh green beans

Colander to drain the green beans

Large skillet

Wide spatula

Small bowl or ramekin

PREPARATION:

Wash and dice the potatoes into small cubes.

If using fresh green beans, cook in a large saucepan of boiling water until crisp-tender, about 3 minutes. Drain and refresh under cold running water.

If using frozen green beans, rinse and drain

Mince garlic

## DIRECTIONS:

Heat oil in a large cast-iron skillet over medium heat until hot enough to sizzle a piece of potato.

Spread potatoes in an even layer and cook, turning every few minutes with a wide spatula, until tender and browned, 15 to 20.

Stir in the green beans, garlic, crushed red pepper, salt and pepper.

Crack each egg into a small bowl and slip them one at a time into the pan on top of the vegetables, spacing evenly.

Cover and cook over medium heat until the whites are set and the yolks are cooked to your taste, 3 to 5 minutes.

Sprinkle the eggs with paprika, if desired, and serve immediately.

## YIELD:

4 Servings

## NUTRITION:

Very High in Vitamin C

# Nutrition Facts

Serving Size 210 g

| Amount Per Serving | |
|---|---|
| Calories 200 | Calories from Fat 74 |
| | % Daily Value* |
| Total Fat 8.2g | 13% |
| Saturated Fat 1.7g | 9% |
| Cholesterol 124mg | 41% |
| Sodium 251mg | 10% |
| Total Carbohydrates 25.8g | 9% |
| Dietary Fiber 4.3g | 17% |
| Sugars 2.3g | |
| Protein 7.1g | |

| | | | |
|---|---|---|---|
| Vitamin A 6% | • | Vitamin C 55% | |
| Calcium 4% | • | Iron 9% | |

Nutrition Grade A
* Based on a 2000 calorie diet

## NOTES:

ⓘ For information about a tip for chopping vegetables, follow this link:
http://www.halleethehomemaker.com/chopping-veg

# CAULIFLOWER & CHEESE CAKES

This is a nice variation from the traditional potato cakes. They serve wonderfully as a side dish, and are even good to take to a potluck to offer a break in the tradition of pots of mac & cheese and green beans.

INGREDIENTS:

1 head cauliflower, cut into florets

$1/4$ cup onion

$1/2$ cup cheddar cheese, shredded

$1/2$ cup panko bread crumbs

2 large eggs, lightly beaten

$1/2$ tsp salt (Kosher or sea salt is best)

$1/4$ tsp cayenne pepper

1 tsp extra virgin olive oil, divided

SUPPLIES:

Large skillet and large pot

Sharp knife/cutting board

Small bowl/whisk or fork

Measuring cups/spoons

Cheese grater

Colander

Spatula

Potato masher or electric mixer

PREPARATION:

Cut the cauliflower into florets.

Chop the onion ①

Shred the cheese

In a small bowl lightly beat the eggs with a whisk or fork.

## DIRECTIONS:

Bring a large pot of water to boil. Add cauliflower and onion and cook for about 10-15 minutes, or until fork tender; drain.

Place in large bowl.

Mash cauliflower with a potato masher or beat with an electric mixer until smooth.

Stir in cheese, panko, eggs, salt, and cayenne pepper. Form cauliflower mixture into 3-inch patties.

In large skillet, heat 1 tablespoon olive oil over medium heat.

Cook the patties in batches, using remaining oil, 4-5 minutes per side, or until golden and set.

Keep warm in oven on low temperature until all batches are finished.

## YIELD:

Serves 6

## NUTRITION:

| Nutrition Facts | |
|---|---|
| Serving Size 95 g | |
| **Amount Per Serving** | |
| Calories 156 | Calories from Fat 83 |
| | % Daily Value* |
| Total Fat 9.2g | 14% |
| Saturated Fat 4.7g | 24% |
| Cholesterol 82mg | 27% |
| Sodium 414mg | 17% |
| Total Carbohydrates 9.7g | 3% |
| Dietary Fiber 1.6g | 7% |
| Sugars 2.1g | |
| Protein 8.9g | |
| Vitamin A 6% • | Vitamin C 35% |
| Calcium 17% • | Iron 6% |
| Nutrition Grade B | |
| * Based on a 2000 calorie diet | |

High in calcium
High in phosphorus
High in selenium
Very high in vitamin B6
Very high in vitamin C

## NOTES:

ⓘ For information about a tip for chopping vegetables, follow this link:
http://www.halleethehomemaker.com/chopping-veg

## FRITTATA PRIMAVERA

I prefer frittatas to omelets. I think they hold much more flavor and carry more substance. You can play around with all sorts of different flavor combinations, adding different vegetables or even some cheeses.

Try this wonderful dinner served with salad and a loaf of crusty French bread.

INGREDIENTS:

1 TBS extra virgin olive oil

1 cup fresh cut asparagus

1 cup fresh mushrooms, chopped

$^1/_2$ cup broccoli florets, chopped

2 scallions, thinly sliced

$^1/_2$ red bell pepper, chopped ⓘ

1 clove garlic, crushed

$^1/_2$ tsp salt (Kosher or sea salt is best)

$^1/_8$ tsp crushed red pepper (optional)

3 whole eggs

3 egg whites

$^1/_4$ cup milk

SUPPLIES:

Large skillet                    Medium sized bowl

Large spatula                   Sharp knife

Whisk                            Cutting board

PREPARATION:

Cut the asparagus into 1-inch pieces

Chop the mushrooms and broccoli

Thinly slice the scallions and bell pepper

Crush the garlic

## DIRECTIONS:

In a large skillet, heat 1 TBS olive oil over medium heat. Add the asparagus, mushrooms, broccoli, scallions, bell pepper, garlic, crushed red pepper, if desired, and salt. Cook for 2 to 3 minutes, or until the vegetables are tender, stirring occasionally.

Meanwhile, in a medium bowl, whisk together the whole eggs, egg whites, and milk. Reduce the heat of the skillet to medium-low and add the egg mixture.

As the mixture begins to set, push the cooked edges slightly toward the center, allowing the liquid to run to the edges of the skillet. Reduce the heat to low, cover, and cook for 8 to 9 minutes, or until the eggs are set.

Slide the frittata onto a serving platter. Cut into 4 wedges and serve immediately.

## NUTRITION:

# Nutrition Facts

Serving Size 108 g

| Amount Per Serving | |
|---|---|
| Calories 80 | Calories from Fat 44 |
| | % Daily Value* |
| Total Fat 4.9g | 8% |
| Saturated Fat 1.1g | 6% |
| Trans Fat 0.0g | |
| Cholesterol 83mg | 28% |
| Sodium 262mg | 11% |
| Total Carbohydrates 3.7g | 1% |
| Dietary Fiber 1.1g | 5% |
| Sugars 2.0g | |
| Protein 6.2g | |
| Vitamin A 14% • | Vitamin C 37% |
| Calcium 4% • | Iron 8% |

Nutrition Grade A
* Based on a 2000 calorie diet

High in riboflavin
Very high in selenium
High in vitamin A
Very high in vitamin B6
Very high in vitamin C

## YIELD:

Serves: 4

## NOTES:

ⓘ For information about a tip for chopping vegetables, follow this link: http://www.halleethehomemaker.com/chopping-veg

# TOMATO, PEPPER, & RICOTTA FRITTATA

This frittata adds the wonderful richness of ricotta cheese, really making this dish a fulfilling meal. Serve it at a brunch or with a salad and crusty French bread for dinner.

### INGREDIENTS:

12 large eggs

$^1/_3$ cup heavy cream

1 $^1/_3$ cups 1 inch cubed bread, crusts removed (day-old is fine)

3 TBS extra virgin olive oil, divided

1 onion, cut into $^1/_2$ inch thick strips

1 each red and green bell peppers, cored, seeded, and cut into $^1/_4$ inch slices

$^1/_2$ cup ripe grape or cherry tomatoes, cut in half

1 TBS unsalted butter

$^1/_3$ cup fresh ricotta

### SUPPLIES:

| | |
|---|---|
| Oven-proof 10-inch skillet | Bread knife |
| Large bowl | Sharp knife |
| Whisk | Cutting board |

### PREPARATION:

Preheat oven to 350° degrees F (175° degrees C).

Remove the crust from the bread and cut it into cubes

Slice the onion into thick strips

Slice the red and green bell peppers

Cut the tomatoes in half

### DIRECTIONS:

In a large bowl, beat eggs, heavy cream, and salt and pepper to taste. Add bread cubes; let soak until softened, about 15 minutes.

Heat 2 tablespoons olive oil in a 10-inch cast-iron skillet over medium heat. Add onion; cook until wilted, about 4 minutes. Add peppers; cook, stirring, until crisp-tender, about 5 minutes. Season with salt and pepper. Stir in tomatoes. Add butter and remaining oil to skillet; heat until foaming. Pour egg and bread mixture into pan; cook over medium without stirring.

Meanwhile, add ricotta by tablespoonfuls, forming little pockets on top. Continue cooking until bottom is lightly browned, about 5 minutes. There should be a few bubbles around edges.

Once bottom crust has formed, transfer skillet to preheated oven; cook until center is firm to touch, about 15–20 minutes.

To serve hot, let frittata stand at room temperature 15 minutes; to serve warm or at room temperature, let stand a little longer.

### YIELD:

Serves: 6

### NUTRITION:

| Nutrition Facts | |
|---|---|
| Serving Size 207 g | |
| **Amount Per Serving** | |
| Calories 307 | Calories from Fat 203 |
| | % Daily Value* |
| Total Fat 22.6g | 35% |
| Saturated Fat 7.6g | 38% |
| Trans Fat 0.0g | |
| Cholesterol 391mg | 130% |
| Sodium 220mg | 9% |
| Total Carbohydrates 10.7g | 4% |
| Dietary Fiber 1.4g | 6% |
| Sugars 3.6g | |
| Protein 14.9g | |
| Vitamin A 41% • | Vitamin C 92% |
| Calcium 12% • | Iron 14% |
| Nutrition Grade B | |
| * Based on a 2000 calorie diet | |

High in selenium
High in vitamin A
Very high in vitamin B6
Very high in vitamin C

### NOTES:

I prefer a purple onion in a fritatta to a white onion.

## Breads & Desserts!

You don't really think "bread" or "dessert" when thinking of an iron skillet. However, the way that the metal conducts the heat evenly can really make a nice crust in breads. And, honestly, there's something about cooking a cake in a skillet that just somehow makes it better.

As I said in the ingredients section of *The Walking Bread*, I use fresh ground grains. I grind them myself.

For cornmeal, I grind popcorn. For wheat, I grind either a combination of hard red and hard white wheats for yeast breads, and soft white wheat for desserts and quick breads. Fresh ground wheat is not the same as store-bought whole wheat flour. It has a finer texture and acts more like white flour in recipes. So, if you don't have fresh-ground flour, you might want to use an unbleached white flour instead of whole wheat. If you prefer whole wheat, then it may be necessary to adjust some of these recipes. Play around with them and see what you can come up with.

Did You know: Cast iron takes longer to warm than other surfaces but retains heat remarkably well and diffuses it evenly.

## HALLEE'S OLD-FASHIONED CORNBREAD

This recipe first appeared in print in my bread cookbook, *The Walking Bread; The Bread Will Rise!* It remains the best traditional cornbread recipe I have ever encountered.

It took me a few years, several brands of cornmeal, and many recipes to finally find one that everyone in my family loved. Now I have friends who ask for "Hallee's cornbread" and friends who come for dinner whose children want to know if they're having "Hallee's Special Cornbread!"

The cornmeal is the most essential ingredient. Since obtaining a grain mill, I grind organic popcorn and use it right away. If you have a mill I strongly recommend this. If not, and you aren't happy with your cornbread, try alternate brands of cornmeal until you hit upon the right one for you.

### INGREDIENTS:

1 cup yellow cornmeal (I once used only *House Autry* brand. Now I grind organic popcorn in my grain mill for fresh cornmeal.)

1 cup flour (I use fresh ground soft white wheat)

1 TBS honey (pure, raw, local honey is always best)

1 tsp salt (Kosher or sea salt is best.)

1 TBS baking powder

2 eggs

1 $\frac{1}{4}$ cup whole milk

4 TBS oil, divided (I don't recommend extra virgin olive oil in this case. Try grapeseed, safflower, or organic canola)

### SUPPLIES:

Cast-iron corn muffin pan or cast-iron skillet

Measuring cups/spoons

mixing bowl

whisk

### PREPARATION:

Put 2 TBS oil in the skillet. Place in oven and turn on to 425° degrees F (220° degrees C). While the oven is heating up, prepare the batter.

### DIRECTIONS:

Mix the dry ingredients. Make a well in the dry batter. Add the wet ingredients and mix, gently, with whisk until smooth. Pour into prepared pan.

Bake 15 to 20 minutes.

### NUTRITION:

| Nutrition Facts | |
|---|---|
| Serving Size 91 g | |

| Amount Per Serving | |
|---|---|
| Calories 215 | Calories from Fat 90 |
| | % Daily Value* |
| Total Fat 10.0g | 15% |
| Saturated Fat 1.8g | 9% |
| Cholesterol 45mg | 15% |
| Sodium 329mg | 14% |
| Potassium 365mg | 10% |
| Total Carbohydrates 27.5g | 9% |
| Dietary Fiber 3.0g | 12% |
| Sugars 4.4g | |
| Protein 5.9g | |
| Vitamin A 3% • | Vitamin C 0% |
| Calcium 14% • | Iron 8% |
| Nutrition Grade B | |
| * Based on a 2000 calorie diet | |

High in manganese
High in phosphorus
High in selenium

### YIELD:

About 12 Servings

### NOTES:

Serve warm with real butter and honey.

# DUTCH OVEN CRUSTY BREAD

This bread is absolutely perfect for dipping into flavored oil. In fact, I've also included the recipe to make the oil. While the bread is rising, make the oil so that it has time for all of the flavors to come together.

**INGREDIENTS:**

### *** FOR THE BREAD: ***

3 cup flour (I use a combination of fresh ground hard red and hard white wheat – see NOTES)

1 tsp baker's yeast from bulk or active dry yeast from packet

1 tsp salt (Kosher or sea salt is best)

1 $^1/_2$ cups warm water

### *** FOR THE ITALIAN DIP: ***

$^1/_2$ cup extra virgin olive oil

2 to 3 tsp dark aged balsamic vinegar, to taste

1 tsp Hallee's Inviting Italian Seasoning ⓘ

fresh basil leaves for garnish, if desired

**SUPPLIES:**

Seasoned cast-iron (or enameled) Dutch oven with lid

Measuring cups/spoons

sifter

3-4 quart mixing bowl with lid (or plastic wrap to seal)

whisk

**PREPARATION:**

Sift the flour at least once, preferably twice

## DIRECTIONS:

Whisk flour, yeast and salt in a 3 to 4 quart bowl with a tight fitting lid. (If you don't have a bowl with a lid, use plastic wrap to seal the bowl.) Add the water and stir with a wooden spoon until the dough is mixed well. The dough will be quite sticky and shaggy looking, but that's okay. Cover the bowl and set aside for 12 to 18 hours (or even up to 24 hours). Overnight is fine.

Preheat oven to 450° degrees F (230° degrees C). Place Dutch oven with the lid into the oven while preheating and heat the pot/lid for 30 minutes. Meanwhile, scrape the risen dough from the bowl onto a heavily floured surface. (Dough will still be very sticky.) DO NOT KNEAD.

With floured hands, gently shape the dough into a round loaf, making sure there's enough flour on the surface so dough doesn't stick. Let the dough just sit there until you're pot is preheated.

Take the hot pot from the oven and gently place the dough into the center of the heated pot. Cover with the lid and return to the oven. Bake for 30 minutes.

Remove the lid and return the pot to the oven for another 10-15 minutes. Gently shake the loaf onto a cooling rack and enjoy the beautiful aroma. Give it a chance to cool before cutting into the loaf.

Make an Italian dip and dip away.

## NUTRITION:

# Nutrition Facts

Serving Size 91 g

Amount Per Serving

| Calories 154 | Calories from Fat 8 |
|---|---|
| | % Daily Value* |
| Total Fat 0.9g | 1% |
| Cholesterol 0mg | 0% |
| Sodium 295mg | 12% |
| Total Carbohydrates 32.8g | 11% |
| Dietary Fiber 5.6g | 22% |
| Protein 6.4g | |

| Vitamin A 0% | • | Vitamin C 0% |
|---|---|---|
| Calcium 2% | • | Iron 10% |

Nutrition Grade A

* Based on a 2000 calorie diet

Very low in saturated fat
No cholesterol
Very low in sugar
High in dietary fiber
Very high in manganese
High in phosphorus
Very high in selenium

**YIELD:**

Makes 1 big crusty loaf

**NOTES:**

I avoid processed flours but you can use unbleached all-purpose flour or bread flour just as easily with this recipe. In fact, if you live at high altitude, you may want to just use bread flour or very well sifted whole wheat flour (sifted at least twice) to get a good light loaf.

Serve with Italian dip, chili, or soup. Also makes a mean garlic bread.

ⓘ I have included a recipe for Hallee's Inviting Italian Seasoning in this cookbook for use when making your own fresh Italian dip.

## IRISH SODA BREAD

❇ 🦪 ✡ 🍬 🌐

No self-respecting cast iron cookbook would be complete without a recipe for Irish Soda Bread. Serve with your favorite corned beef recipe.

**INGREDIENTS:**

2 ¹/₂ cup flour (I use fresh ground soft white wheat)

1 tsp aluminum-free baking powder

¹/₂ tsp baking soda

¹/₂ tsp salt (Kosher or sea salt is best)

2 TBS granulated sugar (or 1 TBS honey, raw local honey is best)

5 TBS unsalted butter, softened

1 TBS caraway seeds

1 cup raisins

³/₄ cup buttermilk ⓘ (See NOTES for possible substitute)

1 egg

(more for dusting skillet and kneading surface)

**SUPPLIES:**

10-inch iron skillet                 Large bowl

Hand mixer or stand mixer            Small bowl

**PREPARATION:**

Preheat oven to 375° degrees F (190° degrees C).

In small bowl, mix buttermilk and egg and set aside.

**DIRECTIONS:**

Generously dust the bottom of a 10 inch iron skillet with flour.

In large bowl or using stand mixer on low speed, combine flour, aluminum-free baking powder, baking soda, salt, and sugar (if using honey instead of sugar, add in next step). Work in butter.

When well combined, slowly add buttermilk and egg mixture until well incorporated (if using honey instead of sugar, add now also).

Add caraway seeds and raisins. Mix.

Batter should be sticky and gooey. Add a bit more milk if too dry.

Remove dough to well floured skillet. Knead slightly if necessary. Usually, just pat down flat very gently, leaving little indents of fingertips (a bit o' Irish love) in dough.

With a very sharp knife, cut an "X" into the top, about $1/8$ to $1/4$ inch deep. Bake at 375° degrees F (190° degrees C) for 50 minutes or until knife comes out of center perfectly clean.

Let cool at least 15 minutes before serving to make it easier to cut/remove from skillet.

YIELD:

Individual yield can be weight or item, depending on the size.

NUTRITION:

## Nutrition Facts

Serving Size 98 g

**Amount Per Serving**

| Calories 273 | Calories from Fat 80 |
|---|---|
| | % Daily Value* |
| Total Fat 8.8g | 14% |
| Saturated Fat 5.0g | 25% |
| Trans Fat 0.0g | |
| Cholesterol 40mg | 13% |
| Sodium 369mg | 15% |
| Total Carbohydrates 45.3g | 15% |
| Dietary Fiber 5.6g | 22% |
| Sugars 14.2g | |
| Protein 7.4g | |

| Vitamin A 5% | • | Vitamin C 1% |
|---|---|---|
| Calcium 10% | • | Iron 11% |

Nutrition Grade B-
* Based on a 2000 calorie diet

High in manganese
High in selenium

NOTES:

ⓘ If you don't have buttermilk, you can use regular whole milk with 1 TBS vinegar added to it. Let it sit for about 5 minutes before using. OR, use regular whole milk without the vinegar and increase baking powder by $1/2$ tsp and omit the baking soda.

## NELLIE THE NURSE NO-KNEAD SKILLET BREAD

# NO-KNEAD SKILLET BREAD

Whoa Nellie! This very simple recipe that makes a flavorful bread. Drizzle with oil and sprinkle with salt and rosemary for an incredible taste.

**INGREDIENTS:**

2 $\frac{1}{4}$ tsp baker's yeast from bulk (1 package active dry yeast)

2 cups lukewarm water

$\frac{1}{2}$ TBS salt (Kosher or sea salt is best)

4 $\frac{1}{3}$ cup flour (I use a combination of fresh ground hard red and hard white wheat)

extra virgin olive oil

rosemary

**SUPPLIES:**

Large bowl

Wooden spoon

10-inch skillet

Measuring cups/spoons

**PREPARATION:**

Combine yeast and warm water in a large bowl or pitcher.

Using a wooden spoon, add 1 cup of flour, then salt, and mix until combined.

Stir in the rest of the flour, one cup at a time, until completely incorporated.

Cover with plastic wrap or a lid that is not shut completely.

Allow to rise for 1 hour.

Preheat the oven to 400° degrees F (205° degrees C).

## DIRECTIONS:

Do not punch down the dough.

Lightly oil the bottom of a cast iron skillet.

Sprinkle a good amount of flour on top of the dough and then cover hands with flour.

Take all of the dough and shape into a disk. (it will be sticky)

Place in the skillet, cover loosely with a towel, and allow to rise for another 30 minutes.

Drizzle a little more oil over the top of the bread, and slash the dough creating an "X" with a knife.

Sprinkle with coarse salt and rosemary leaves.

Bake for 35-40 minutes until the top is a deep brown color.

## YIELD:

Individual yield can be weight or item, depending on the size.

## NUTRITION:

| Nutrition Facts | |
|---|---|
| Serving Size 98 g | |
| **Amount Per Serving** | |
| Calories 273 | Calories from Fat 80 |
| | % Daily Value* |
| Total Fat 8.8g | 14% |
| Saturated Fat 5.0g | 25% |
| Trans Fat 0.0g | |
| Cholesterol 40mg | 13% |
| Sodium 369mg | 15% |
| Total Carbohydrates 45.3g | 15% |
| Dietary Fiber 5.6g | 22% |
| Sugars 14.2g | |
| Protein 7.4g | |
| Vitamin A 5% • | Vitamin C 1% |
| Calcium 10% • | Iron 11% |
| Nutrition Grade B- | |
| * Based on a 2000 calorie diet | |

High in Manganese
High in selenium

## NOTES:

This is the perfect bread to go with a hearty stew or soup.

SUN GIRL BROWN SUGAR & WALNUT SKILLET CAKE

# BROWN SUGAR & WALNUT SKILLET CAKE ❄ ⏱ 🐚 🍶

When I decided to make this cake, it took less time to make the batter than it took to preheat the oven. You use a whisk to make it, not a mixer, which means you can whip it up in little time and the cleanup is very easy. It's a delicious, dense cake – almost like a Beautiful Blondie ①.

### INGREDIENTS:

1 cup flour (I use fresh ground soft white wheat)

$\frac{1}{4}$ tsp aluminum-free baking powder

Pinch of salt (Kosher or sea salt is best)

2 large eggs

$\frac{1}{2}$ cup brown sugar

$\frac{1}{2}$ cup granulated sugar

1 stick unsalted butter, melted

$\frac{1}{2}$ cup walnuts

### SUPPLIES:

Measuring cups/spoons

Large bowls/Whisk

9-inch skillet

Sharp knife/cutting board

### PREPARATION:

Chop the walnuts

Melt the butter

Preheat the oven to 350° degrees F (175° degrees C).

Heavily butter a 9-inch cast-iron skillet.

### DIRECTIONS:

In a large bowl, whisk together the flour, baking powder, and salt.

In another bowl, whisk the eggs and sugar together. Add the butter and whisk until satiny. Stir in the flour mixture; whisk until smooth. Spread batter in the skillet and top with walnuts.

Bake 25 to 30 minutes, or until a toothpick inserted in the center of the cake comes out clean. Serve slightly warm or at room temperature.

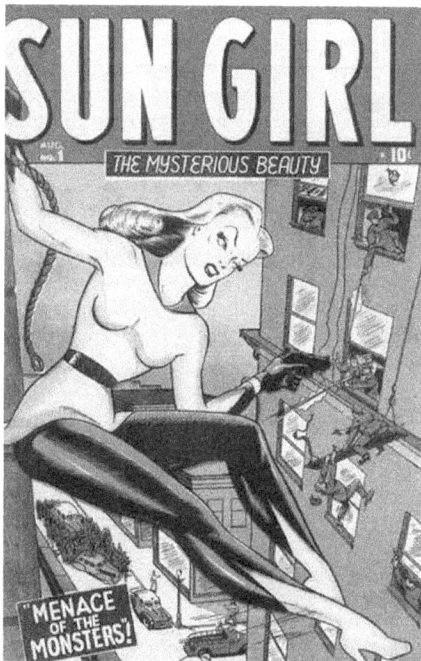

**YIELD:**

Makes 8 servings

**NUTRITION:**

# Nutrition Facts

Serving Size 72 g

Amount Per Serving

| Calories 306 | Calories from Fat 158 |
|---|---|
| | % Daily Value* |
| Total Fat 17.5g | 27% |
| Saturated Fat 8.0g | 40% |
| Trans Fat 0.0g | |
| Cholesterol 77mg | 26% |
| Sodium 135mg | 6% |
| Total Carbohydrates 34.2g | 11% |
| Dietary Fiber 0.9g | 4% |
| Sugars 21.5g | |
| Protein 5.2g | |

| Vitamin A 8% | • | Vitamin C 0% |
|---|---|---|
| Calcium 3% | • | Iron 7% |

Low in sodium
High in Vitamin A

**NOTES:**

This cake is wonderful served alone, or with a light whipped cream.

ⓘ For a great recipe for Beautiful Homemade Blondies, follow this link: http://www.halleethehomemaker.com/beautiful-blondies/

IRON SKILLET MAN SAYS...

To avoid getting smudges on all your kitchen towels, designate one to use exclusively for drying your cast-iron skillet.

## CORN CAKE WITH STEWED CHERRIES

It is kind of surprising how amazing this cornmeal cake tastes with the cherry sauce on top. Serve this as a "company's coming" dessert for a nice change from the usual chocolate cakes

### INGREDIENTS:

1 cup flour (I use fresh ground soft white wheat)

1 tsp aluminum-free baking powder

$^3/_4$ tsp salt (Kosher or sea salt is best)

6 TBS cornmeal

2 large eggs, plus 1 large egg yolk

$^2/_3$ cup whole milk

2 TBS unsalted butter

$^1/_2$ cup extra virgin olive oil

20 oz frozen cherries

1 lemon to make 2 tsp lemon peel zest and $^1/_4$ cup lemon juice

1 $^1/_2$ cups granulated sugar

### SUPPLIES:

| | |
|---|---|
| Two 10-inch cast iron skillets | Measuring cups/spoons |
| Large bowl | Colander to rinse cherries |
| Medium bowl | Citrus zester |
| Sifter | Juicer |
| Whisk | Wooden spoon |

### PREPARATION:

Place a 10-inch cast-iron skillet in the oven and preheat the oven to 350°F (175° degrees C).

Zest a lemon for the lemon zest and juice the lemon for the juice

Rinse and drain cherries

### DIRECTIONS:

In a medium bowl, sift together the flour, baking powder and salt. Stir in the cornmeal. In a separate medium bowl whisk together the eggs, egg yolk, milk, olive oil and lemon zest until frothy. Add 3/4 cup of the sugar and whisk to combine.

Pour the wet ingredients over the dry ingredients and mix just until the batter is smooth. Swirl the butter in the hot cast-iron pan until melted, then pour the batter into the skillet. Return the pan to the oven and cook until the center is set, about 25 minutes.

While the cake bakes, set a 10-inch skillet over high heat and add the cherries, lemon juice, the remaining 3/4 cup sugar and cook until the cherries have released most of their juice, 10 to 12 minutes. Remove from the heat and set aside until ready to use.

Allow the cake to cool 5 minutes before serving. Slice it into wedges and serve with the stewed cherries spooned over the top.

### YIELD:

Serves 8.

### NUTRITION:

| Nutrition Facts | | |
|---|---|---|
| Serving Size 190 g | | |
| **Amount Per Serving** | | |
| Calories 417 | Calories from Fat 169 | |
| | | % Daily Value* |
| Total Fat 18.8g | | 29% |
| Saturated Fat 4.7g | | 24% |
| Cholesterol 82mg | | 27% |
| Sodium 268mg | | 11% |
| Potassium 288mg | | 8% |
| Total Carbohydrates 62.8g | | 21% |
| Dietary Fiber 3.7g | | 15% |
| Sugars 45.2g | | |
| Protein 5.9g | | |
| Vitamin A 17% | • | Vitamin C 17% |
| Calcium 8% | • | Iron 10% |
| Nutrition Grade B- | | |
| * Based on a 2000 calorie diet | | |

High in Vitamin A
High in Vitamin C

NOTES:

This is really good with some whipped cream as well as the stewed cherries on top.

# HONEY CORN CAKES ❄ ⏱ 🌿

These are so amazing. I serve them with honey and butter mixed together. You will eat them until you feel like you could never eat another bite.

## INGREDIENTS:

1 10-ounce package frozen organic corn

$^1/_2$ cup whole milk

$^1/_4$ cup honey (pure, raw, local honey is always best)

3 eggs

1 cup flour (I use fresh ground soft white wheat)

$^1/_2$ tsp garlic salt

extra virgin olive oil

## SUPPLIES:

Colander for rinsing corn

Measuring cups/spoons

Large bowl

Whisk

Skillet

spatula

## PREPARATION:

Rinse and drain the corn

## DIRECTIONS:

Combine corn, milk, honey, eggs, flour, and garlic salt. Whisk together until smooth.

Lightly coat a large skillet with olive oil; heat to medium temperature. Pour $^1/_3$ cup portions of corn mixture into skillet and cook 1 $^1/_2$ to 2 minutes on each side.

YIELD:

Serves 4

NUTRITION:

## Nutrition Facts

Serving Size 187 g

Amount Per Serving

| Calories 308 | Calories from Fat 45 |
|---|---|
| | % Daily Value* |
| Total Fat 5.0g | 8% |
| Saturated Fat 1.6g | 8% |
| Cholesterol 126mg | 42% |
| Sodium 68mg | 3% |
| Potassium 136mg | 4% |
| Total Carbohydrates 58.1g | 19% |
| Dietary Fiber 2.5g | 10% |
| Sugars 23.4g | |
| Protein 10.8g | |

| Vitamin A 4% | • | Vitamin C 8% |
|---|---|---|
| Calcium 6% | • | Iron 12% |

Nutrition Grade B+

* Based on a 2000 calorie diet

Low in Sodium
High in selenium

NOTES:

ⓘ Corn is in the "dirty dozen", and is likely a GMO product if it's NOT organic. So, I only use organic corn products.

# BIG APPLE PANCAKE

This is a fun dessert or a weekend breakfast. Dust with powdered sugar, or top with cinnamon whipped cream. Kids will love helping you make this recipe.

**INGREDIENTS:**

1 large sweet apple, peeled, cored, and cut into $1/4$ inch wedges

$1/2$ cup whole milk

2 TBS unsalted butter

$1/2$ cup flour (I use fresh ground soft white wheat)

4 eggs

3 TBS granulated sugar

$1/2$ tsp pure vanilla extract ① (see NOTES)

$1/4$ tsp salt (Kosher or sea salt is best)

confectioners' sugar for garnish

**SUPPLIES:**

Large skillet

Blender (or food processor)

Sharp knife/cutting board

**PREPARATION:**

Position rack in oven's center and preheat to 450° degrees F (230° degrees C).

Peel and core apple. Cut into $1/4$ inch wedges

**DIRECTIONS:**

Melt butter in a medium skillet over medium heat, then transfer 1 TBS melted butter to a blender. Add apple wedges to skillet and cook, turning once, until they start to soften, about 3 to 5 minutes. Arrange wedges around edge.

Meanwhile, mix milk, flour, eggs, sugar, vanilla, and salt with butter in blender or stand mixer until batter is smooth. Pour over apples and transfer skillet to oven. Bake for 15 minutes, or until pancake is puffed and golden. Dust with confectioners' sugar and serve immediately.

YIELD:

Servings 4

NUTRITION:

| Nutrition Facts | |
|---|---|
| Serving Size 152 g | |
| **Amount Per Serving** | |
| Calories 242 | Calories from Fat 103 |
| | % Daily Value* |
| Total Fat 11.4g | 18% |
| Saturated Fat 5.6g | 28% |
| Trans Fat 0.0g | |
| Cholesterol 182mg | 61% |
| Sodium 263mg | 11% |
| Potassium 215mg | 6% |
| Total Carbohydrates 28.0g | 9% |
| Dietary Fiber 2.9g | 12% |
| Sugars 15.8g | |
| Protein 8.6g | |
| Vitamin A 9% • | Vitamin C 3% |
| Calcium 7% • | Iron 8% |

High in selenium

NOTES:

Gala or Golden apples work especially well in this recipe.

Serving suggestion: Set out bowls of these toppings and let your guests customize their plates.

- ✓ Real maple syrup
- ✓ Real whipped cream
- ✓ Organic vanilla yogurt
- ✓ Chopped walnuts or pecans
- ✓ Dried cranberries
- ✓ Cinnamon sugar

ⓘ For information about how easy and economical it is to make your own homemade vanilla extract, follow this link

http://www.halleethehomemaker.com/homemade-vanilla

## EASY WHOLE WHEAT APPLE FRITTERS

I made these for breakfast one Sunday morning, and my kids asked for them all week long. They were incredibly easy to make and tasted amazing.

### INGREDIENTS:

1 $^1/_4$ cup whole wheat flour (I use fresh-ground soft white wheat)

$^1/_3$ cup sugar

1 tsp aluminum-free baking powder

$^1/_4$ tsp salt (Kosher or Sea salt is best)

1 $^1/_2$ tsp ground cinnamon

$^1/_4$ tsp. nutmeg

$^1/_2$ tsp. vanilla extract

1 TBS unsalted butter

1 egg

$^1/_3$ cup whole milk

1 $^1/_2$ cups chopped apple

1 cup powdered sugar

2 TBS whole milk

oil for frying (I use grapeseed oil or organic canola oil)

### SUPPLIES:

Large bowl & spoon

Measuring cups/spoons

Sharp knife/cutting board

Deep skillet

Slotted spoon

Paper towel lined plate

Small bowl & spoon

Wire rack

PREPARATION:

Peel and chop the apples.

Melt the butter.

Fill skillet with about 1-inch oil. Heat oil in skillet to 375° F (190° C)

Mix the powdered sugar and the 2 TBS milk in a small bowl. Set aside.

DIRECTIONS:

Mix the dry ingredients in the large bowl. Make a well in the center. Add the milk, egg, melted butter, and vanilla.

Stir until just mixed (do not use a whisk – the dough is really thick). Gently stir in the apples. (There is going to seem as much apples as there is dough – this is a good thing).

Test the oil by dropping a single water drop into the oil. If it skitters on the top, it's ready.

Place a spoonful of the batter in the oil (about the size of a golf ball). Add spoonfuls until you have 4 or 5 fritters in the oil. Don't overcrowd the oil.

Using the slotted spoon, carefully remove the fritters to the paper towel.

After a minute or two, roll each fritter in the powdered sugar.

Place on the wire rack to cool and dry.

YIELD:

Makes 8 servings

NUTRITION:

# Nutrition Facts

Serving Size 104 g

Amount Per Serving

Calories 255 — Calories from Fat 87

% Daily Value*

| | |
|---|---|
| Total Fat 9.7g | 15% |
| Saturated Fat 2.1g | 10% |
| Trans Fat 0.0g | |
| Cholesterol 26mg | 9% |
| Sodium 99mg | 4% |
| Potassium 128mg | 4% |
| Total Carbohydrates 40.8g | 14% |
| Dietary Fiber 3.0g | 12% |
| Sugars 26.0g | |
| Protein 3.8g | |

| | | |
|---|---|---|
| Vitamin A 2% | • | Vitamin C 2% |
| Calcium 3% | • | Iron 5% |

Low in sodium
High in manganese

NOTES:

Coconut oil would be wonderful to use to fry these fritters.

## ORANGE DROP DOUGHNUTS

I discovered this recipe when I had doughnuts on the menu one morning but hadn't set yeast doughnut dough to rise. It's a quick and easy, sweet breakfast food that your family will love.

INGREDIENTS:

2 oranges to create $\frac{1}{2}$ cup orange juice and 2 TBS grated orange rind

2 eggs

$\frac{1}{2}$ cup sugar

$\frac{1}{4}$ tsp Kosher salt

Grapeseed oil for frying

2 TBS coconut oil

2 cups whole wheat flour

2 tsp baking powder

SUPPLIES:

skillet

zester

Bowl/wooden spoon

juicer

## PREPARATION:

Zest orange.

Juice the oranges.

Fill a skillet with oil until you have an inch of oil in the pan.

Heat skillet to 375° degrees F.

## DIRECTIONS:

Beat the eggs. Beat in sugar and coconut oil.

Sift together the dry ingredients.

Mix together the orange juice and orange rind.

Add the dry ingredients to the egg mixture alternately with the orange juice. Stir just until moistened.

Drop by spoonfuls into the hot oil. The dough will drop down, then rise to the surface as it cooks. When it's brown on one side, gently flip over and brown the other side.

Remove from the oil with a slotted spoon and drain. Sprinkle with powdered sugar.

## NUTRITION:

# Nutrition Facts

Serving Size 83 g

| Amount Per Serving | |
|---|---|
| Calories 276 | Calories from Fat 105 |
| | % Daily Value* |
| Total Fat 11.6g | 18% |
| Saturated Fat 4.0g | 20% |
| Cholesterol 41mg | 14% |
| Sodium 91mg | 4% |
| Potassium 209mg | 6% |
| Total Carbohydrates 39.0g | 13% |
| Dietary Fiber 1.1g | 4% |
| Sugars 14.0g | |
| Protein 4.7g | |
| Vitamin A 1% | Vitamin C 25% |
| Calcium 7% | Iron 11% |
| Nutrition Grade B | |
| * Based on a 2000 calorie diet | |

Low in sodium
High in selenium
No Trans Fats

YIELD:

Makes 8 servings

NOTES:

Coconut oil would be wonderful to use to fry these doughnuts.

You can glaze these instead of sprinkling with sugar. Add $1/3$ cup boiling water to 1 cup powdered sugar and mix well. Dip the warm doughnut into the glaze.

## CHURROS

This is my family's traditional breakfast for Christmas morning. It's a very light dough, crispy, with a delicate sweet flavor brought about by sprinkling it with sugar and cinnamon. I only make them for Christmas so that we have something different and new to look forward to every year.

### INGREDIENTS:

### *** CHURRO:

1 cup water

$^{1}/_{4}$ cup unsalted butter

1 TBS sugar

$^{1}/_{4}$ tsp salt (Kosher or sea salt is best)

1 cup fresh ground whole wheat flour (I use soft white)

2 eggs

Organic cold pressed grapeseed oil for frying

### *** DUSTING:

$^{1}/_{2}$ cup sugar

1 tsp cinnamon

### SUPPLIES:

heavy 2-quart pot

wooden spoon

cookie sheets

waxed paper

pastry bag with large star tip

skillet

paper towels

slotted spoon

PREPARATION:

line cookie sheets with waxed paper

Mix $\frac{1}{2}$ cup sugar with cinnamon.

DIRECTIONS:

Bring water, butter, sugar, and salt to a boil. Add the flour. Stir vigorously until the mixture forms a ball that doesn't separate.

Cool for 10 minutes. Add the eggs, 1 at a time, and beat with wooden spoon until smooth.

Spoon dough into pastry bag fitted with a large star tip. Pipe the dough into strips 2-3 inches long onto waxed paper lined cookie sheet.

Freeze strips about 20 minutes or until firm.

While the strips are in the freezer, heat the oil to 375° degrees F .

Drop the strips into the oil, a few at a time. Fry 3-4 minutes or until browned. Remove from oil with slotted spoon and put on paper towel lined plate. Immediately sprinkle with sugar/cinnamon mixture.

YIELD:

Makes 8 servings

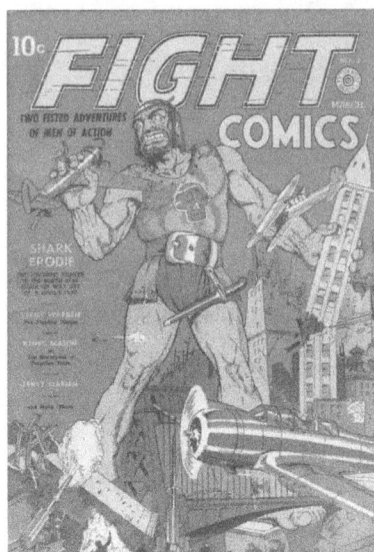

NUTRITION:

## Nutrition Facts

Serving Size 71 g

| Amount Per Serving | |
|---|---|
| Calories 183 | Calories from Fat 125 |
| | % Daily Value* |
| Total Fat 13.9g | 21% |
| Saturated Fat 4.7g | 23% |
| Cholesterol 56mg | 19% |
| Sodium 116mg | 5% |
| Potassium 77mg | 2% |
| Total Carbohydrates 12.5g | 4% |
| Dietary Fiber 1.8g | 7% |
| Sugars 1.6g | |
| Protein 3.5g | |

| | | |
|---|---|---|
| Vitamin A 5% | • | Vitamin C 0% |
| Calcium 1% | • | Iron 4% |

Nutrition Grade B-
* Based on a 2000 calorie diet

High in selenium
High in manganese
No Trans Fats

NOTES:

You could also drizzle with honey in lieu of dusting with sugar. Coconut oil would be wonderful to use to fry these fritters.

You can prepare the dough and pipe out the churros then freeze them overnight so that all you have to do in the morning is heat up the oil.

## WHOLE WHEAT SOPAPILLAS

I have a good friend who asked me to make whole wheat sopapillas, so I spent some time finding a way to make fried dough appeal to all of us "real food" minded mamas. Sopapilla means "little pillow" and can be used in a savory dish much like a tortilla or a pita bread. For this dish, I used them as a breakfast bread and drizzled them with honey. They were beyond amazing. A wonderful breakfast to kick off a *Cinco de Mayo* celebration.

INGREDIENTS:

2 cups whole wheat flour (I used soft white berries)

1 tsp aluminum-free baking powder

$^1/_2$ tsp salt (Kosher or sea salt is best)

2 TBS extra virgin coconut oil

$^3/_4$ cup warm water

extra virgin coconut oil for frying

SUPPLIES:

Large bowl & spoon

measuring cups/spoons

pastry cutter or fork

rolling pin

pizza cutter or sharp knife/cutting board

Deep skillet

Slotted spoon

Paper towel lined plate

PREPARATION:

Put enough coconut oil in your pan so that you will have about an inch of oil.

Heat to just over medium heat.

## DIRECTIONS:

Mix flour, baking powder, and salt. Cut in coconut oil until the mixture resembles fine crumbs. Stir in water.

Let rest for about 10 minutes.

Roll to about $^1/_4$ inch thick. Using a pizza cutter or a sharp knife, cut into squares.

Gently slide a couple of pieces at a time into the hot oil.

Cook until browned (about 2 minutes.) The dough will puff up. Gently turn over and cook an additional minute or until the other side is browned.

Remove from oil and drain on paper towels.

Drizzle with honey.

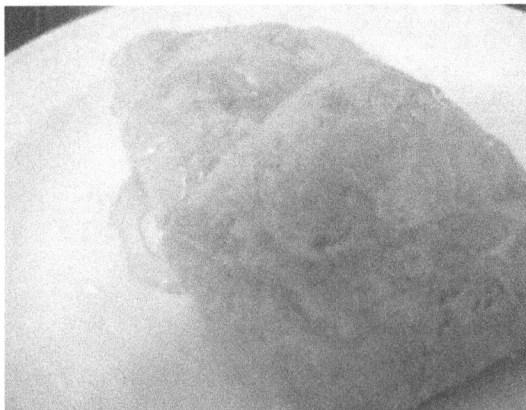

**YIELD:**

About 12 pieces.

**NUTRITION:**

## Nutrition Facts

Serving Size 38 g

Amount Per Serving

| Calories 90 | Calories from Fat 24 |
|---|---|
| | % Daily Value* |
| Total Fat 2.7g | 4% |
| Saturated Fat 2.1g | 10% |
| Trans Fat 0.0g | |
| Cholesterol 0mg | 0% |
| Sodium 99mg | 4% |
| Potassium 124mg | 4% |
| Total Carbohydrates 14.7g | 5% |
| Dietary Fiber 2.4g | 10% |
| Protein 2.7g | |

| Vitamin A 0% | • | Vitamin C 0% |
|---|---|---|
| Calcium 3% | • | Iron 5% |

Nutrition Grade B+

* Based on a 2000 calorie diet

No cholesterol
Very low in sugar
High in selenium
High in thiamin

**NOTES:**

These are best if served immediately.

SEASONINGS, SAUCES, SOUPS, AND SUCH

# Extras!

In coming up with so many of my favorite skillet recipes for this cookbook, I discovered that I rely on a lot of whole food, real food, clean food seasoning mixes, soups, and sauces to bring these meals to life. I make these seasoning mixes fresh and keep them on hand in my spice cabinet year round.

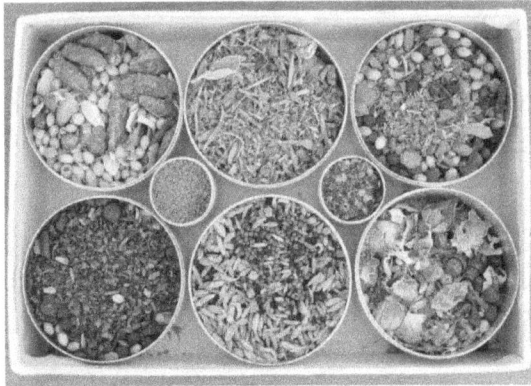

This section is all about flavor and convenience. The seasoning mixes you'll find here are especially useful in all kinds of recipes. Try adding just a dash more or less of certain spices in your own personalized combinations to create your own signature flavors.

It is so easy and economical to make these and such a money saver, you may never buy overpriced store bought blends again. Best of all, there is nothing better than knowing 100% of the ingredients you are using in your cooking and knowing for certain that you are only using real food. You control the amount of salt and you can purposefully exclude potentially harmful ingredients like GMOs or MSG.

IRON SKILLET MAN SAYS...

To avoid getting smudges on all your kitchen towels, designate one to use exclusively for drying your cast-iron skillet.

# MONTREAL STEAK SEASONING RECIPE ⏱ ✝ 🌶 ✡ 🌾 🌐

According to multiple sources, Schwart's Montreal Hebrew Delicatessen is credited with the creation of Montreal steak seasoning. The story goes that a Schwartz's broilerman by the name of Morris "The Shadow" Sherman, during the 1940s and 1950s began adding the deli's smoked meat pickling spices to his own rib and liver steaks. It didn't take long before customers began asking for the seasoning as well. Due to its popularity, it eventually became a norm in most Montreal delis and steakhouses.

Montreal steak seasoning is a true North American invention that combines the British love of beefsteaks with the French flair for seasoning. It's excellent on red meats like steaks as well as on sides like baked potatoes.

INGREDIENTS:

2 TBS paprika

1 TBS crushed coriander

1 TBS garlic powder (not garlic salt)

1 TBS onion powder

1 TBS dill

1 TBS crushed red pepper flakes

2 TBS freshly ground black pepper

OPTIONAL

1 TBS salt (Kosher salt is best)

## SUPPLIES:

shaker, spice jar, or other container like a small Mason jar for finished mix

mortar with pestle OR a coffee grinder OR a food processor OR a blender

## PREPARATION:

You will need some means to crush and combine the seasoning once mixed.

If you have a mortar and pestle you can prepare this seasoning in a very artisan fashion. An electric coffee grinder works great and a food processor or a blender will also suffice.

## DIRECTIONS:

If making a **MONTREAL STEAK RUB:**

Combine 2 tablespoons paprika, 2 tablespoons crushed black pepper, 1 tablespoon granulated garlic, 1 tablespoon granulated onion, 1 tablespoon crushed coriander, 1 tablespoon dill, and 1 tablespoon crushed red pepper flakes.

If making a **MONTREAL STEAK SEASONING:**

Add 1 tablespoon kosher salt.

For either: Mix all ingredients well. Briefly grind with a mortar and pestle or use a coffee grinder, a food processor, or a blender and just pulse a few times.

## NUTRITION:

| Nutrition Facts | |
|---|---|
| Serving Size 51 g | |
| **Amount Per Serving** | |
| Calories 149 | Calories from Fat 31 |
| | % Daily Value* |
| Total Fat 3.4g | 5% |
| Saturated Fat 0.6g | 3% |
| Cholesterol 0mg | 0% |
| Sodium 25mg | 1% |
| Total Carbohydrates 32.4g | 11% |
| Dietary Fiber 11.7g | 47% |
| Sugars 6.6g | |
| Protein 6.8g | |
| Vitamin A 195% • | Vitamin C 35% |
| Calcium 18% • | Iron 52% |
| * Based on a 2000 calorie diet | |

Very high in dietary fiber
Very high in iron
Very high in manganese
Very high in vitamin A
Very high in vitamin B6
Very high in vitamin C
High in magnesium
High in phosphorus
High in potassium
High in riboflavin
High in calcium
Low in saturated fat
Very low in sodium
No cholesterol

**YIELD:**

About $^3/_4$ cup

**NOTES:**

As a time saver, I keep some premade spice mixes on-hand for various recipes. This one keeps well in an airtight container and I have never found a more tasty rub for red meat dishes.

Store at room temperature in an airtight container away from light. Use within three months.

I really recommend leaving off the salt in this mix. When you leave out the salt, you still have a tasty and delicious seasoning and an always ready dry rub.

## HALLEE'S PREMADE POULTRY RUB RECIPES

There are a just few poultry seasonings I really like and I decided to share them both. There is no salt in these recipes. Salt wicks moisture (water) from your bird and that is almost never what you want. You want a bird that is juicy and moist, not dry. It's best to season your bird dishes with salt to your personal taste *after* your bird is fully cooked. The absence of salt means that these seasonings can also safely act as rubs for red meats or fish if you like.

The first recipe is paprika based and, while it is a traditional continental poultry seasoning, Americans will relate it more with southwestern or southern dishes. It is especially good as a rub if you are roasting, broiling, or popping an entire bird in the rotisserie oven.

The second recipe is probably what most people in North America think of as the most traditional kind of poultry seasoning we grew up with. It is a sage based seasoning but the main flavor kick comes from the marjoram. This seasoning mix is light in color and goes well in traditional soups, stews, and especially in stuffings. In fact, if you are making a savory cornbread, you should be sure not to leave this out. I have included some optional ingredients that I have found fill out the flavor of this seasoning especially if you are making a bird for a holiday meal.

Combine the two of these together in a 2:1 ratio and as the seasoning base for your southern fried chicken before you apply a thick buttermilk batter and you are in for flavors the Colonel himself would have envied.

INGREDIENTS:

### POULTRY SEASONING MIX 1:

3 tsp paprika

3 tsp dry mustard

3 tsp onion powder

1 tsp garlic powder

1 tsp thyme

$\frac{1}{2}$ tsp basil

1 $\frac{1}{2}$ tsp fresh ground white pepper

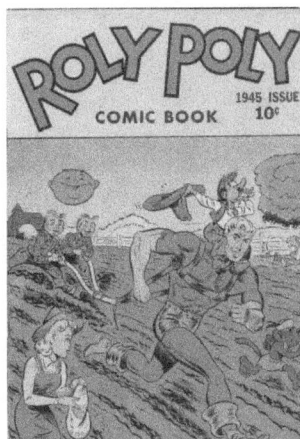

## POULTRY SEASONING MIX 2:

1 TBS sage

1 TBS marjoram

2 TBS parsley flakes

1 TBS oregano

1 TBS thyme

1 TBS rosemary

1 TBS celery leaves

1 TBS fresh ground white pepper

OPTIONAL (for holiday meals)

1 TBS ginger

1 tsp fresh ground nutmeg

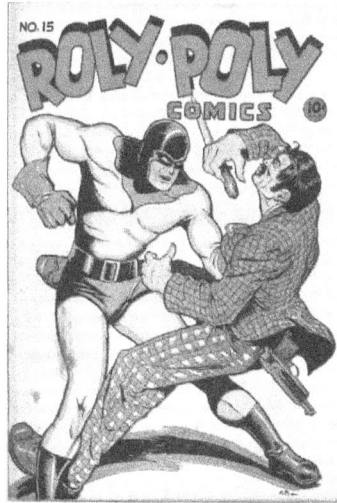

**SUPPLIES:**

measuring cups/spoons

shaker, clean empty spice jar, or other small airtight container like a small Mason jar for finished mixes

MAY NEED: mortar & pestle / coffee grinder / food processor / blender

MAY NEED: zester or very fine grater if grating fresh nutmeg

**PREPARATION:**

You may need some means to crush and combine the seasoning once mixed depending on the coarseness or fineness you desire to personally achieve.

If you have a mortar and pestle you can prepare these seasoning mixes in a very artisan fashion. An electric coffee grinder works great and a food processor or a sturdy blender will also suffice.

**DIRECTIONS:**

For each recipe, mix all ingredients well. If desired, briefly grind with a mortar and pestle or use a coffee grinder, a food processor, or a blender and just pulse a few times until your personally desired consistency has been achieved.

**YIELD:**

Each yields about 30-35 grams or about $^1/_5$ cup

NUTRITION:

## POULTRY SEASONING MIX 1:

| Nutrition Facts | |
|---|---|
| Serving Size 31 g | |
| **Amount Per Serving** | |
| Calories 110 | Calories from Fat 35 |
| | % Daily Value* |
| Total Fat 3.9g | 6% |
| Cholesterol 0mg | 0% |
| Sodium 9mg | 0% |
| Total Carbohydrates 17.5g | 6% |
| Dietary Fiber 5.7g | 23% |
| Sugars 4.6g | |
| Protein 5.0g | |
| Vitamin A 68% • | Vitamin C 13% |
| Calcium 12% • | Iron 27% |
| * Based on a 2000 calorie diet | |

Low in saturated fat
No cholesterol
Very low in sodium
High in calcium
Very high in dietary fiber
Very high in iron
High in manganese
High in magnesium
High in phosphorus
Very high in selenium
Very high in vitamin A
Very high in vitamin B6
High in vitamin C

## POULTRY SEASONING MIX 2:

| Nutrition Facts | |
|---|---|
| Serving Size 36 g | |
| **Amount Per Serving** | |
| Calories 63 | Calories from Fat 16 |
| | % Daily Value* |
| Total Fat 1.8g | 3% |
| Saturated Fat 0.7g | 3% |
| Cholesterol 0mg | 0% |
| Sodium 18mg | 1% |
| Total Carbohydrates 13.8g | 5% |
| Dietary Fiber 7.9g | 32% |
| Sugars 0.6g | |
| Protein 2.3g | |
| Vitamin A 29% • | Vitamin C 31% |
| Calcium 27% • | Iron 59% |
| * Based on a 2000 calorie diet | |

No cholesterol
Low in sodium
Very high in calcium
Very high in dietary fiber
Very high in iron
Very high in manganese
Very high in magnesium
High in potassium
Very high in vitamin A
High in vitamin B6
Very high in vitamin C

NOTES:

These poultry seasoning mixes keep well in airtight containers and it is nearly always a welcome surprise how good and fresh they smell when opening them to use in a recipe here and there. Store at room temperature in an airtight container away from light. Keeps well for up to three months.

These size well so feel free to double, triple, or quadruple the ingredients.

# ITALIAN SEASONING (OR RUB)

When reading the first four ingredients to this mix, if the old song that goes, "Parsley, sage, rosemary, and thyme" doesn't get stuck in your head, then you probably think I am REALLY old. These four herbs in various ratios are the foundation for any Italian seasoning and this recipe is no exception.

I typically make my seasoning mixes in the summertime when my fresh herbs are taking over the world and I always have more than I can possibly use. I just lay my herbs out on a baking sheet lined with parchment and low bake them in the oven or, if it isn't otherwise in use, I'll put them in the dehydrator. In a few hours I have fresh dried herbs. I usually pulse them in the food processor or coffee grinder until they reach the desired consistency. A blender works also, just not as well.

If you aren't using fresh herbs, you can just mix store bought dried herbs together. No need to grind them. But store bought herbs seem to have a better flavor when you grind them right before using them. Likely it releases some of the remaining essential oils.

This mix is a perfect rub. It's great on chicken, pasta, or even as a dipping sauce when mixed with a little extra virgin olive oil for crusty bread.

INGREDIENTS:

***4 REQUIRED INGREDIENTS***

1 TBS dried flat leaf Italian parsley

1 TBS dried sage

1 TBS dried rosemary

1 TBS dried thyme

***OPTIONAL OR TO TASTE***

1 TBS dried basil

1 TBS dried oregano

1 TBS dried marjoram

1 TBS fresh ground white pepper

***OPTIONAL IF MAKING A SEASONING MIX***

$1/2$ TBS salt (Kosher salt is best)

## SUPPLIES:

measuring spoons

air tight shaker, spice jar, or other air tight container like a small Mason jar for finished mix

possibly mortar with pestle OR a coffee grinder OR a food processor OR a blender

## PREPARATION:

If you have a mortar and pestle you can prepare this seasoning in a very artisan fashion. You may need some means to crush the ingredients once combined.

An electric coffee grinder works great and a food processor or a blender will also suffice.

## DIRECTIONS:

If making an ITALIAN SEASONING:

Start with $^1/_2$ TBS Kosher salt. Then:

If making a ITALIAN RUB skip the above and:

Combine 1 TBS dried basil, 1 TBS dried marjoram, 1 TBS dried oregano, 1 TBS dried rosemary, 1 TBS dried sage, 1 TBS dried thyme, 1 TBS dried flat leaf Italian parsley, 1 TBS fresh ground white pepper.

Mix all ingredients well. If using fresh dried herbs, briefly grind with a mortar and pestle or use a coffee grinder, food processor, or blender and just pulse a few times.

Store at room temperature in an airtight container away from light. This recipe mix keeps well in an airtight container for up to 3 months in a cool dry cabinet.

YIELD:

$^{1}/_{2}$ cup (8 Tablespoons)

NUTRITION:

| Nutrition Facts | |
|---|---|
| Serving Size 3 g | |
| **Amount Per Serving** | |
| Calories 8 | Calories from Fat 2 |
| | % Daily Value* |
| Total Fat 0.2g | 0% |
| Cholesterol 0mg | 0% |
| Sodium 1mg | 0% |
| Total Carbohydrates 1.7g | 1% |
| Dietary Fiber 1.0g | 4% |
| Protein 0.3g | |
| Vitamin A 3% • | Vitamin C 3% |
| Calcium 3% • | Iron 7% |
| * Based on a 2000 calorie diet | |

No cholesterol
Very low in sodium
Low in sugar
Very high in calcium
Very high in dietary fiber
Very high in iron
Very high in manganese
Very high in magnesium
High in potassium
Very high in vitamin A
High in vitamin B6
Very high in vitamin C

NOTES:

If there is a particular flavor you don't care for, simply leave it out. Don't like basil? Don't add it. Oregano not your thing? Leave it out or substitute a different fresh herb that is to your liking. Personally, I almost always leave out the pepper. If I want or need pepper, I prefer to just add fresh ground black pepper right on the spot.

I really recommend leaving off the salt in this mix. When you leave out the salt, you still have a tasty and delicious seasoning and an always ready dry rub.

## ORIENTAL SEASONING RECIPE

The ingredients that come in a packet of Oriental Seasoning mix with Ramen noodles or the shakers you buy off the shelf are often packed with things no human being should eat. From monosodium glutamate to hydrogenated oils.

This seasoning mix not only serves as a great marinade but also uses good ingredients that will make your normally over salty and somewhat hum-drum Ramen noodles sing a happy tune.

### INGREDIENTS:

1 cup soy sauce (Tamari or fermented soy sauce strongly preferred)

$^1/_3$ cup light unsulfured molasses

2 TBS ground ginger

2 TBS dry mustard

1 tsp garlic powder

$^1/_2$ tsp onion powder

### SUPPLIES:

measuring cups/spoons

small mason jar with lid or other air tight container

### PREPARATION:

A small mason jar is ideal for both mixing and storing this seasoning.

### DIRECTIONS:

In a jar with a screw top lid combine soy sauce, molasses, ginger, mustard, garlic powder, and onion powder. Shake vigorously to mix.

Store, covered, in the refrigerator for up to six weeks.

Use this seasoning in place of Oriental Seasoning packets that come with Ramen noodles or as a marinade for burgers, steak or chops.

### YIELD:

About 1 $^1/_3$ cup

NUTRITION:

| Nutrition Facts | |
|---|---|
| Serving Size 40 g | |
| **Amount Per Serving** | |
| Calories 61 | Calories from Fat 6 |
| | **% Daily Value*** |
| Total Fat 0.7g | 1% |
| Cholesterol 0mg | 0% |
| Sodium 1442mg | 60% |
| Total Carbohydrates 11.9g | 4% |
| Dietary Fiber 0.7g | 3% |
| Sugars 6.8g | |
| Protein 2.3g | |
| Vitamin A 0% • | Vitamin C 0% |
| Calcium 4% • | Iron 8% |
| * Based on a 2000 calorie diet | |

Very low in saturated fat

No cholesterol

High in iron

Very high in manganese

High in magnesium

High in potassium

High in selenium

High in vitamin B6

NOTES:

As a time saver, I keep premade spice mixes on-hand for various recipes. This one keeps well in an airtight container for up to six months.

## CHINESE 5-SPICE SEASONING

Many authentic Oriental recipes call for Chinese 5-spice. This is an incredibly easy-to-put-together spice mixture that stores well in a mason jar with a lid.

### INGREDIENTS:

1 tsp ground cloves

1 tsp ground cinnamon

1 tsp ground star anise

1 tsp fennel seed, toasted then ground if necessary

1 tsp Szechuan peppercorns, toasted then ground if necessary

### SUPPLIES:

Measuring spoons

small mason jar with lid or other air tight container

### PREPARATION:

You may need to first lightly toasted then grind your Szechuan peppercorns if you purchased them fresh. This will give them an amazing flavor.

A small mason jar is ideal for both mixing and storing this seasoning.

### DIRECTIONS:

The recipe sizes very well.

Size proportionally.

Mix the spices together and store any leftover in an airtight jar.

### YIELD:

5 tsp

NUTRITION:

| Nutrition Facts | |
|---|---|
| Serving Size 40 g | |
| **Amount Per Serving** | |
| Calories 61 | Calories from Fat 6 |
| | % Daily Value* |
| Total Fat 0.7g | 1% |
| Cholesterol 0mg | 0% |
| Sodium 1442mg | 60% |
| Total Carbohydrates 11.9g | 4% |
| Dietary Fiber 0.7g | 3% |
| Sugars 6.8g | |
| Protein 2.3g | |
| Vitamin A 0% • | Vitamin C 0% |
| Calcium 4% • | Iron 8% |
| * Based on a 2000 calorie diet | |

Very low in saturated fat

No cholesterol

High in iron

Very high in manganese

High in magnesium

High in potassium

High in selenium

High in vitamin B6

NOTES:

As a time saver, I keep some premade spice mixes on-hand for various recipes. This one keeps well in an airtight container for up to six months.

## CAJUN-CREOLE SEASONING

This Cajun-Creole seasoning blend is MSG-free and can be made salt free simply by leaving off the optional salt. It is excellent for seasoning rice, meats, soups and stews, or anything that needs a flavor boost. I have never found a more authentic tasting essence for Cajun or Creole inspired dishes.

**INGREDIENTS:**

5 TBS paprika

2 TBS onion powder

2 TBS garlic powder

2 TBS dried oregano

2 TBS dried basil

1 TBS dried thyme

1 TBS cayenne pepper

1 TBS fresh ground white pepper

1 TBS fresh ground black pepper

**OPTIONAL**

3 TBS salt (Kosher salt is best)

**SUPPLIES:**

measuring spoons

air tight shaker, spice jar, or other air tight container like a small Mason jar for finished mix

mortar with pestle OR a coffee grinder OR a food processor OR a blender

**PREPARATION:**

You will need some means to crush the ingredients once combined.

If you have a mortar and pestle you can prepare this seasoning in a very artisan fashion.

An electric coffee grinder works great and a food processor or a blender will also suffice.

## DIRECTIONS:

If making a CAJUN/CREOLE SEASONING:

Start with 3 tablespoon Kosher salt. Then:

If only making a CAJUN/CREOLE RUB then skip the above and:

Combine 5 tablespoons paprika, 2 tablespoons onion powder, 2 tablespoons garlic powder, 2 tablespoons dried oregano, 2 tablespoons dried basil, 1 tablespoon dried thyme, 1 tablespoon cayenne pepper, 1 tablespoon fresh ground white pepper, 1 tablespoon fresh ground black pepper. Then:

Mix all ingredients well. Briefly grind with a mortar and pestle or use a coffee grinder, a food processor, or a blender and just pulse a few times. Store at room temperature in an airtight container away from light.

## YIELD:

About ²/₃ cup

## NUTRITION:

| Nutrition Facts | |
|---|---|
| Serving Size 100 g | |
| **Amount Per Serving** | |
| Calories 289 | Calories from Fat 65 |
| | % Daily Value* |
| Total Fat 7.2g | 11% |
| Saturated Fat 1.4g | 7% |
| Cholesterol 0mg | 0% |
| Sodium 34mg | 1% |
| Total Carbohydrates 61.5g | 21% |
| Dietary Fiber 25.1g | 100% |
| Sugars 13.6g | |
| Protein 12.8g | |
| Vitamin A 429% • | Vitamin C 72% |
| Calcium 39% • | Iron 114% |
| * Based on a 2000 calorie diet | |

Very high in vitamin C
Very high in vitamin B6
Very high in vitamin A
Very high in manganese
Very high in iron
Very high in dietary fiber
High in riboflavin
High in potassium
High in phosphorus
High in niacin
High in magnesium
High in calcium
Very low in sodium
No cholesterol

## NOTES:

I really recommend leaving off the salt. When you leave out the salt, you still have a tasty and delicious seasoning and an always ready dry rub. This mix keeps well in an airtight container and may be stored for up to 3 months in a cool dry cabinet.

## SHERRY-GINGER ASIAN SAUCE

Need a great tasting light stir-fry sauce to team with your favorite wok meals? Look no further than this awesome Sherry-Ginger Asian Sauce.

### INGREDIENTS:

4 TBS sherry or port ⓘ (see NOTES for substitute)

8 tsp cornstarch

4 tsp soy sauce (Tamari or fermented soy sauce strongly preferred)

$\frac{1}{2}$ tsp ground ginger

### SUPPLIES:

measuring cups/spoons

mixing bowl/whisk OR sports cup with blender ball

### PREPARATION:

ⓘ If using a substitute for sherry, mix your substitute juice.

### DIRECTIONS:

In a small bowl, whisk all ingredients OR use a sports cup with a blender ball. Mix until cornstarch is smooth and completely dissolved. Stir again before using.

### NUTRITION:

| Nutrition Facts | |
|---|---|
| Serving Size 78 g | |
| Amount Per Serving | |
| Calories 136 | Calories from Fat 1 |
| | % Daily Value* |
| Total Fat 0.1g | 0% |
| Cholesterol 0mg | 0% |
| Sodium 1343mg | 56% |
| Total Carbohydrates 21.8g | 7% |
| Protein 2.7g | |
| Vitamin A 0% • | Vitamin C 0% |
| Calcium 1% • | Iron 4% |
| * Based on a 2000 calorie diet | |

Very low in saturated fat

No cholesterol

Low in sugar

YIELD:

Makes just over $^1/_2$ cup

NOTES:

ⓘ If you abstain from alcohol even in cooking, you can substitute a 100% pure grape juice (ensure there is no apple juice in it) and one tsp of distilled vinegar to approximate the same flavor and properties while cooking.

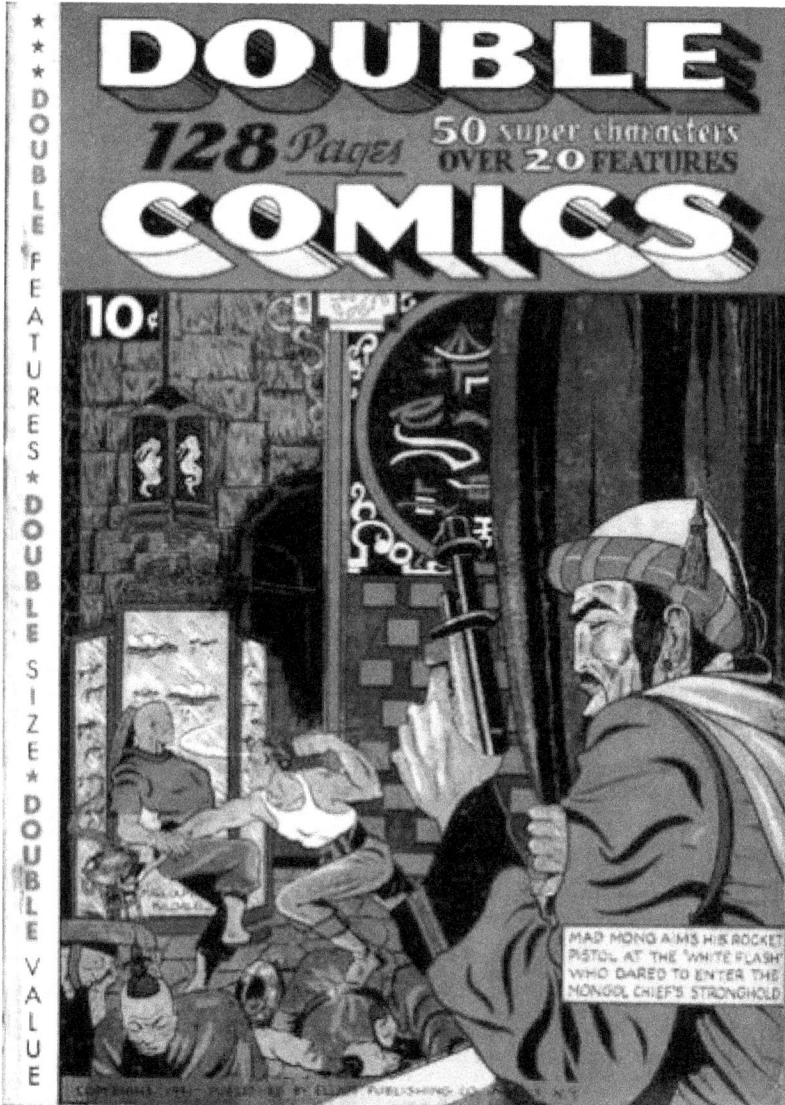

## RED MEAT MARINADE

On "low" red meat cuts like plate, flank, skirt, shank, and even some rounds, you might want to tenderize the meat with a mallet or hammer or use a meat tenderizer that punctures the meat with dozens of sharp needles, then place it in a really good marinate to baste and soak for a day or two prior to cooking.

The marinade will further tenderize and deeply infuse the otherwise often plain cuts with delightful and unique flavor.

 INGREDIENTS:

3 TBS dried basil

1 ¹/₂ TBS dried parsley flakes

1 ¹/₂ TBS garlic powder

¹/₂ cup extra virgin olive oil

¹/₃ cup soy sauce (Tamari or fermented soy sauce strongly preferred)

¹/₃ cup fresh lemon juice

¹/₄ cup Worcestershire sauce

1 tsp minced garlic

1 tsp fresh ground white pepper

¹/₄ tsp your favorite hot pepper sauce (optional)

 SUPPLIES:

Airtight container to store the marinating meat

food processor OR a blender

PREPARATION:

No special preparation is needed

YIELD:

1 ³/₄ cup

## DIRECTIONS:

Place the minced garlic, soy sauce, extra virgin olive oil, lemon juice, Worcestershire sauce, garlic powder, basil, parsley, and white pepper in a food processor or blender. Add your favorite hot pepper sauce if desired.

In a food processor pulse several times. In a blender, blend on high speed for 30 seconds until thoroughly mixed.

Pour marinade over desired type of meat. Cover, and refrigerate for at least 8 hours and up to 2 days.

Cook meat as desired.

## NUTRITION:

| Nutrition Facts | |
|---|---|
| Serving Size 98 g | |

| Amount Per Serving | |
|---|---|
| Calories 261 | Calories from Fat 229 |
| | % Daily Value* |
| Total Fat 25.4g | 39% |
| Saturated Fat 3.8g | 19% |
| Trans Fat 0.0g | |
| Cholesterol 0mg | 0% |
| Sodium 1369mg | 57% |
| Total Carbohydrates 8.1g | 3% |
| Dietary Fiber 0.8g | 3% |
| Sugars 4.6g | |
| Protein 2.2g | |
| Vitamin A 5% • | Vitamin C 21% |
| Calcium 2% • | Iron 5% |
| * Based on a 2000 calorie diet | |

Very low in sodium

No cholesterol

## NOTES:

If you don't abstain, you can add one half cup of dry red wine to this marinate when intended for red meats and one half cup of dry white wine when marinating any kind of bird.

I prefer to prepare this in my blender though I have done it both ways. From a blender, it pours easier when mixed and seems like an easier cleanup afterward.

## ROASTED GARLIC ORANGE MAYONNAISE 🕙 ✝ 🐚 🌾 🌐

Roasted garlic mayonnaise adds a really unique flavor to a number of chicken and seafood dishes. Make your own homemade mayonnaise with farm fresh eggs and organic grapeseed oil. Add an orange juice syrup and you have a signature flavor that sings with sweet citrus and smoky roasted garlic flavor.

### INGREDIENTS:

1 cup Hallee's Homemade Mayonnaise ⓘ

1 cup fresh orange juice

1 large head garlic, outer papery layer removed

salt (Kosher or sea salt is best), to taste

freshly ground black pepper, to taste

### SUPPLIES:

measuring cups/spoons

heavy saucepan

aluminum foil

### PREPARATION:

Prepare the orange juice up to a day in advance.

Preheat oven to 350° degrees F (175° degrees C).

### DIRECTIONS:

Place orange juice in a small, heavy saucepan and bring to a boil. Reduce heat to medium and simmer until the juice is thick and syrupy, about 20 to 25 minutes, watching it carefully so it does not burn. Cool and refrigerate until needed. (Makes ¼ cup.)

Rub the head of the garlic a bit in your hands and remove some of the papery outer sheath. Another technique is to place the head in an empty quart mason jar and shake it like a maraca.

Now, using a very sharp knife, slice the top ¼ inch off the top of the garlic exposing the tips of the individual cloves. Place the garlic in the middle of a 1 foot by 1 foot sheet of aluminum foil. Rub the bulb entirely with 1 tsp of extra virgin olive oil, then wrap tightly in the foil.

Place the wrapped garlic head on a baking sheet or pie pan and roast for about 1 hour to 1 hour and 15 minutes at 350° degrees F (175° degrees C) or until the bulb is very soft when pierced with a fork.

Remove from the oven and let cool slightly. When cool enough to handle, break off the cloves and squeeze or press the cloves at the base to push the pulp out into a small bowl or ramekin. Add 2 to 3 tablespoons of the reduced orange juice. Using a fork, smash the garlic pulp into a paste to fully blend with the orange juice syrup. Stir well.

When well mixed, fold in the mayonnaise. When well mixed, lightly season with salt and pepper, as desired. Taste and adjust the seasonings.

Transfer to an airtight container, seal, and refrigerate until needed – or at least 6 hours – to allow the flavors to fully blend.

### YIELD:

Makes about 1 cup, enough for 8 servings.

### NUTRITION:

| Nutrition Facts | |
|---|---|
| Serving Size 90 g | |
| **Amount Per Serving** | |
| Calories 185 | Calories from Fat 119 |
| | % Daily Value* |
| Total Fat 13.2g | 20% |
| Saturated Fat 1.9g | 10% |
| Cholesterol 10mg | 3% |
| Sodium 281mg | 12% |
| Total Carbohydrates 16.8g | 6% |
| Sugars 6.1g | |
| Protein 1.2g | |
| Vitamin A 3% • | Vitamin C 39% |
| Calcium 3% • | Iron 2% |
| * Based on a 2000 calorie diet | |

Low in cholesterol

Very high in vitamin C

### NOTES:

Serve as an accompaniment to tuna steaks, salmon patties, or on fish tacos. Try it with roasted chicken breast or on your favorite burger.

ⓘ For the recipe to my homemade mayonnaise, follow this link:
http://www.halleethehomemaker.com/homemade-mayonnaise

## HALLEE'S HEAVENLY HOMEMADE KETCHUP

Ketchup, Catsup – however you spell it, this is an incredibly flavorful condiment. Catsup is a very simple condiment with just a few ingredients. Either one will contain tomato, onion, salt, and cinnamon. Ketchup will also contain additional seasonings and something sweet like brown sugar.

Ketchup is the perfect base for homemade sauces, like Kelly's BBQ Sauce. It's easy, perfectly flavored, and keeps well.

If you're set on making your own steak sauce, this is also the recipe you will need! See the optional ingredients and NOTES section for details.

INGREDIENTS:

12 to 13 pounds of garden fresh ripe tomatoes (about 8 quarts)

10 medium apples

10 medium onions

2 inch stick cinnamon

2 long red peppers

2 cups apple cider vinegar

$^3/_4$ cup brown sugar, packed

1 whole nutmeg

2 TBS Kosher or pickling salt

1 TBS paprika

1 TBS whole allspice

1 TBS whole celery seed

1 TBS cloves

1 TBS mace

1 TBS black peppercorns

1 clove garlic

2 small bay leaves

$^1/_2$ tsp dry mustard

**OPTIONAL (steak sauce):**

$^1/_2$ cup dark raisins (see NOTES)

$^3/_4$ cup apple cider vinegar

SUPPLIES:

really large stock pot (or sauce pan) with lid

miniature grater or zester for the nutmeg

sharp knife/cutting board

cheesecloth or muslin for a spice bag, string to tie bag

measuring cups/spoons

mesh strainer or food mill

water bath canner

mason jars/lids

canning funnel for ladling sauce into jars

ladle

PREPARATION:

Wash tomatoes and cut into small pieces.

Peel, core, and slice apples.

Slice onions.

Grate the nutmeg.

Chop the garlic.

Remove seeds and membranes of peppers (you may want to wear gloves when handling peppers and remember not to rub your eyes)

Tie in cheesecloth or muslin bag: allspice, celery seed, cloves, mace, and peppercorns.

DIRECTIONS:

Simmer tomatoes, onions, peppers, and apples in large stock pot until soft.

Strain through a mesh strainer or food mill and return to the pot.

Add the spice bag, paprika, cinnamon, nutmeg, dry mustard, garlic, and bay leaves.

Boil rapidly without scorching, stirring often, about 1 $\frac{1}{2}$ hours or until thick and reduced to half.

In the meantime, bring water in your water bath canner to a boil, and sterilize your jars and lids in the boiling water, boiling for 20 minutes. Remove just prior to filling with the sauce so that the jars are hot when you fill them.

Remove spice bag and cinnamon.

Add vinegar and salt.

Simmer and adjust salt to taste. Boil 10 minutes longer until thick.

Wash your hands thoroughly. Carefully ladle into sterilized hot jars. Wipe the rims with a clean towel or clean paper towels. Seal. Place in the water bath canner and boil for 20 minutes. Remove. When cool, check to make sure all lids have sealed properly before storing.

YIELD:

About 5 to 6 quarts

NUTRITION:

## Nutrition Facts

Serving Size 110 g

Amount Per Serving

| Calories 36 | Calories from Fat 2 |
|---|---|
| | % Daily Value* |
| Total Fat 0.2g | 0% |
| Trans Fat 0.0g | |
| Cholesterol 0mg | 0% |
| Sodium 203mg | 8% |
| Total Carbohydrates 8.1g | 3% |
| Dietary Fiber 1.7g | 7% |
| Sugars 5.4g | |
| Protein 0.9g | |

| Vitamin A 2% | • | Vitamin C 32% |
|---|---|---|
| Calcium 1% | • | Iron 7% |

* Based on a 2000 calorie diet

Very low in saturated fat

No cholesterol

High in dietary fiber

High in iron

High in manganese

High in potassium

Very high in vitamin B6

Very high in vitamin C

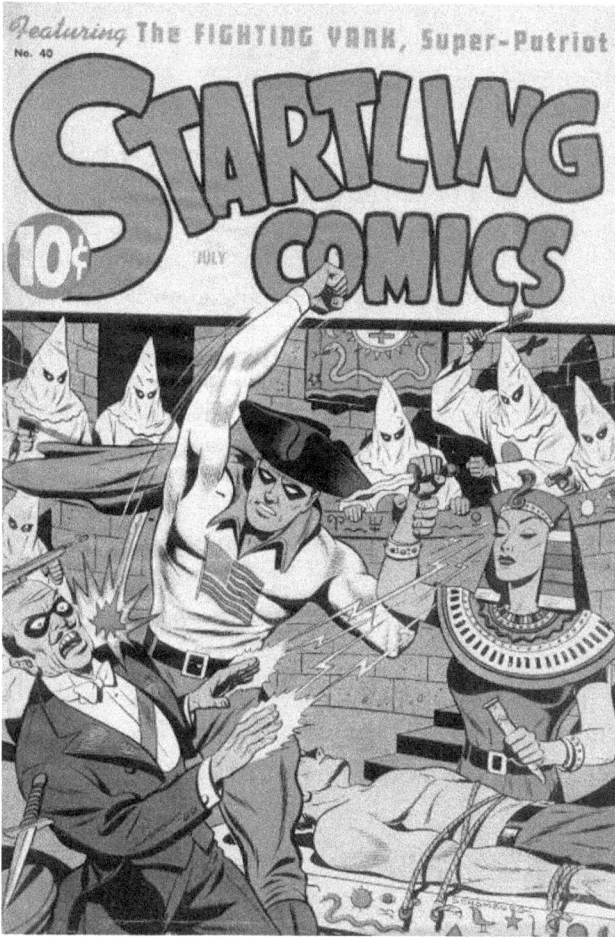

**NOTES:**

This recipe makes a lot of Ketchup! But it also sizes well. Cut the ingredients exactly in half or by three quarters to evenly yield less product.

Try this!

Reconstitute $\frac{1}{2}$ cup dark raisins in $\frac{3}{4}$ cup apple cider vinegar. The ideal way to do this is to combine them in a small crock pot and cook on low for 6 to 8 hours. Once the raisins are reconstituted, blend them into a raisin paste in a blender or food processor. Add this raisin paste to the remainder of 1 quart of this Ketchup recipe and mix very well before canning. Congratulations! You just made "traditional steak sauce" with the most rich body and flavor you can imagine.

## KELLY'S HOMEMADE BBQ SAUCE ✳ ✝ 🐚 ✡ ℘ 🍬

Kelly Moeggenborg a.k.a. Kelly the Kitchen Kop has been a 'politically incorrect' voice for Real Food in the spirit of the Weston A. Price foundation since launching her popular blog in 2008. Visit her amazing website at http://kellythekitchenkop.com/ for even more Real Food ideas. Pick up her *Real Food Ingredient Guide* also available from House of Bread Books™.

Kelly's recipe for homemade barbecue sauce is absolutely the best, hands down, I have ever tried. I have never had any store bought or restaurant barbecue sauce come even close to beating it. It's easy, perfectly flavored, and keeps well.

### INGREDIENTS:

$1/4$ cup honey (pure, raw, local honey is always best) or brown sugar

24 oz Hallee's Homemade organic ketchup or 1 standard size bottle

3 TBS soy sauce (Tamari or fermented soy sauce strongly preferred)

2 TBS raw apple cider vinegar

2 TBS stone ground mustard (not Dijon)

Juice from 2 organic lemons

$1/2$ tsp onion powder

$1/2$ tsp paprika

$1/4$ tsp Kosher or sea salt — do not use iodized salt!

**OPTIONAL:**

about $1/4$ cup to $1/2$ cup purple raisins (see NOTES)

### SUPPLIES:

You need a big mixing bowl or else a stand mixer makes short work of this recipe.

Use glass jars to store the leftover sauce if possible. Plastic generally does not keep the sauce well since it is porous.

## PREPARATION:

This makes a lot of sauce, you may want to halve the recipe. Mix it up well, do lots of taste testing and play around with it until you like it.

## DIRECTIONS:

Mix all the ingredients and taste. Add small amounts of whatever is needed until the taste suits you.

## YIELD:

Individual yield can be weight or item, depending on the size.

## NUTRITION:

High in selenium

| Nutrition Facts | |
|---|---|
| Serving Size 92 g | |
| **Amount Per Serving** | |
| Calories 170 | Calories from Fat 54 |
| | % Daily Value* |
| Total Fat 6.0g | 9% |
| Saturated Fat 1.0g | 5% |
| Cholesterol 29mg | 10% |
| Sodium 363mg | 15% |
| Total Carbohydrates 23.7g | 8% |
| Dietary Fiber 0.7g | 3% |
| Sugars 3.5g | |
| Protein 5.3g | |
| Vitamin A 1% • | Vitamin C 1% |
| Calcium 10% • | Iron 8% |
| * Based on a 2000 calorie diet | |

## NOTES:

This is great on hot-wings, too. It's perfect for any barbecue flavor dish.

Try this! Reconstitute about $\frac{1}{4}$ cup to $\frac{1}{2}$ cup raisins in some of the vinegar. Once they are reconstituted, blend into a raisin paste and add to this recipe. This will give the sauce a much more "traditional steak sauce" type flavor and add some rich body to the sauce.

## HOMEMADE CROCK POT STOCKY BIRD BROTH ❋ ✡ 𝄐 🍷 🍲

Never know what to do with the leftover bird carcass after a holiday meal? Hearty bone stocks and bone broths are the perfect solution. You can also freeze your chicken, duck, goose, squab, or other game bird carcasses until you have enough on hand to make a broth.

The vegetables need not be absolutely fresh. In fact, making stocks regularly is a great way to clean out the pantry shelves and crisper drawers to use up all your supplies without waste. Slightly wilted celery or carrots and somewhat dry onions or garlic cloves, or those barely wrinkled potatoes that are just starting to sprout may not be something you would proudly serve up at a Sunday potluck – but all of them make a perfectly fine stock provided they aren't actually spoiled.

Make stock or broth and freeze it in 1-cup increments. I use breast milk storage bags ⓘ to freeze my broth. They are sterile, freezer safe, the perfect size, and have measurement marks right on them like a measuring cup. Then, when you need a cup of stock or broth, just pull it out of the freezer, defrost, and use it.

INGREDIENTS:

**For a stock, you will only need:**

1 turkey carcass, (or a few smaller bird carcasses) need not be intact

skin and any remaining giblets (in other words, the bones, meat bits, skin, any part of the bird you don't care to eat)

2 cups dry white wine ⓘ

6 cloves garlic

4 stalks of celery, with leaves

4 carrots

3 onions

1 TBS whole black peppercorns

$\frac{1}{2}$ tsp basil

$\frac{1}{2}$ tsp parsley

water to cover

**If you are making a broth, add:**

3 tsp each of Kosher or sea salt and 1 tsp fresh ground black pepper. Add any other herbs, spices, or seasonings of your choice to taste.

SUPPLIES:

Sharp knife/cutting board

Saucepan with lid or crock pot

Measuring cups/spoons

Mesh strainer

PREPARATION:

Peel then roughly chop the carrots.

Halve the garlic.

Roughly chop the celery.

Quarter the onion

DIRECTIONS:

Place all of the ingredients in the crock pot and cook on low for 6 hours.

-OR-

Place all of the ingredients in the saucepan. Bring to a boil. Cover and simmer on low for several hours.

Strain the broth with the mesh strainer.

Freeze.

Use in any recipe that calls for turkey or chicken broth or turkey or chicken stock.

 YIELD:

6 quarts

 NUTRITION:

| Nutrition Facts | |
|---|---|
| Serving Size 1 cup (8 fl oz) (244 g) | |
| Per Serving | % Daily Value* |
| Calories 10 | |
| Calories from Fat 5 | |
| Total Fat 0.6g | 1% |
| Saturated Fat 0.1g | 1% |
| Polyunsaturated Fat 0.2g | |
| Monounsaturated Fat 0.2g | |
| Cholesterol 0mg | 0% |
| Sodium 764mg | 32% |
| Potassium 15mg | 0% |
| Carbohydrates 0.7g | 0% |
| Dietary Fiber 0.0g | 0% |
| Sugars 0.7g | |
| Protein 0.7g | |
| Vitamin A 0% · Vitamin C 0% | |
| Calcium 1% · Iron 0% | |

No cholesterol

High in calcium

High in magnesium

Very high in selenium

 NOTES:

If you are making a broth, each time you skim, sample the liquid and add salt, pepper, and any other herbs and spices you like to taste. Fresh ground pepper is always best. Kosher or sea salt is best. Iodized salt can add too much iodine to the mixture.

To make a hearty vegetable stock or broth, just leave out the bird and up the amount and variety of vegetables. The process is identical.

ⓘ For information about freezing in breast milk bags, check out this link: http://www.halleethehomemaker.com/2010/05/the-perfect-solution-for-freezing-broth/

ⓘ If you abstain from alcohol even in cooking, you can substitute a 100% pure grape juice (ensure there is no apple juice in it) and one teaspoon of distilled vinegar to approximate the same flavor and properties while cooking.

## HOMEMADE STOCKY CROCK POT BEEF BROTH

❄ ✡ 🚫 🍷 🍲

The health benefits of bone stocks and broths are really not in question among whole food, real food enthusiasts. Making your own stocks and broths ensures that you control all of the ingredients which is a very good thing since store bought stocks and broths often contain MSG and other industrial grade chemicals.

The vegetables needed to make a good stock or broth need not be absolutely fresh. In fact, making stocks regularly is a great way to clean out the pantry shelves and crisper drawers to use up all your supplies without waste. Slightly wilted celery or carrots and somewhat dry onions or garlic cloves, or those barely wrinkled potatoes that are just starting to sprout may not be something you would proudly serve up at a Sunday potluck – but all of them make a perfectly fine stock provided they aren't actually spoiled.

Make this beef broth and freeze it in 1 cup increments. I use breast milk storage bags ① to freeze my broth. They are sterile, freezer safe, the perfect size, and have measurement marks right on them like a measuring cup. Whenever you need beef broth or beef stock, just pull it out of the freezer and defrost it.

INGREDIENTS:

**For a stock, you will only need:**

1 large beef soup bone -AND/OR- 1 pound beef trimmings (whatever is on hand)

6 cups filtered water

1 TBS gluten-free soy sauce (Tamari or fermented soy sauce strongly preferred)

3 carrots

2 celery ribs (with leaves)

1 small onion

4 medium fresh white mushrooms

2 small bay leaves

1 tsp dried parsley

1/2 tsp garlic powder

$^{1}/_{4}$ tsp paprika

1 pinch ground thyme

2 cups dry red wine ⓘ

**If you are making a broth, add:**

salt and pepper to taste (Kosher or sea salt is best/fresh ground pepper is best) and other herbs and seasonings of choice to taste

SUPPLIES:

crock pot (or saucepan with lid)

sharp knife/cutting board

measuring cups/spoons

mesh strainer

PREPARATION:

Peel then roughly chop the carrots.

Roughly chop the celery.

Quarter the onion

Halve the mushrooms

DIRECTIONS:

Place all of the ingredients in crock pot and cook on low for 6 hours, skimming occasionally.

-OR-

Place all of the ingredients in the saucepan. Bring to a boil. Reduce heat. Cover and simmer on low for several hours, skimming occasionally.

Strain the solids from the stock with the mesh strainer.

Freeze.

 YIELD:

6 cups

 NUTRITION:

| Nutrition Facts | |
|---|---|
| Serving Size 155 g | |
| **Amount Per Serving** | |
| Calories 136 | Calories from Fat 45 |
| | % Daily Value* |
| Total Fat 5.0g | 8% |
| Saturated Fat 2.1g | 10% |
| *Trans* Fat 0.0g | |
| Cholesterol 41mg | 14% |
| Sodium 447mg | 19% |
| Total Carbohydrates 6.0g | 2% |
| Dietary Fiber 1.8g | 7% |
| Sugars 2.6g | |
| Protein 17.4g | |
| Vitamin A 106% | Vitamin C 7% |
| Calcium 3% | Iron 16% |

High in iron

Very high in vitamin A

Very high in vitamin B6

 NOTES:

If making a stock, do not salt at all. If making a broth, each time you skim, sample the liquid and add salt, pepper, and any other herbs and spices you like to taste. Remember that Kosher or sea salt is best. Iodized salt can add too much iodine to the mixture. Fresh ground pepper is always best.

To make a hearty vegetable stock or broth, just leave out the bird and up the amount and variety of vegetables. The process is identical.

ⓘ  For information about freezing in breast milk bags, check out this link: http://www.halleethehomemaker.com/2010/05/the-perfect-solution-for-freezing-broth/

ⓘ  If you abstain from alcohol even in cooking, you can substitute a 100% pure grape juice (ensure there is no apple juice in it) and one teaspoon of distilled vinegar to approximate the same flavor and properties while cooking.

## "CAN-DO" NO CANS CREAM OF MUSHROOM SOUP

I don't know why it took me so long to start making my own cream of mushroom soup. I use it in many different casserole dishes. I was out of the canned soup one day while making a family favorite recipe and decided, rather than run to the store, to make my own. The recipe came out perfectly – the flavors were spot-on.

Using fresh mushrooms and your own broth, you can make it without using a can-opener even once.

**INGREDIENTS:**

1 cup chopped mushrooms (fresh or 2 4-ounce cans)

1 $^{1}/_{2}$ cups whole milk

$^{1}/_{2}$ cup heavy cream

2 cups broth ( chicken, turkey, or vegetable broth, I use Hallee's Heavenly Homemade turkey broth)

3 TBS unsalted butter (if using fresh mushrooms, add 1 more TBS butter)

2 TBS flour (I used fresh ground whole wheat)

1 tsp grated onion

1 tsp paprika

1 tsp Kosher or sea salt

$^{1}/_{8}$ tsp fresh ground black pepper

**SUPPLIES:**

heavy saucepan

food processor or sharp knife/cutting board

cheese grater

wooden spoon

whisk

measuring cups/spoon

**PREPARATION:**

If you're using fresh mushrooms, chop them. In a skillet, saute them in 1 TBS butter over medium heat until soft.

If you're using canned mushrooms, drain them and process them in the food processor.

Grate the onion

**DIRECTIONS:**

Melt butter over medium heat in saucepan. Whisk in the flour, salt, and pepper.

When it gets bubbly, whisk in the milk, cream, and broth.

Bring to a boil. Boil for 1 minute.

Stir in mushrooms and onion. Stir in paprika.

Cook, stirring regularly, for 10 minutes.

Remove from heat.

**YIELD:**

6 Servings

**NUTRITION:**

| Nutrition Facts | |
|---|---|
| Serving Size 102 g | |
| **Amount Per Serving** | |
| Calories 83 | Calories from Fat 62 |
| | % Daily Value* |
| Total Fat 6.9g | 11% |
| Saturated Fat 4.2g | 21% |
| Trans Fat 0.0g | |
| Cholesterol 21mg | 7% |
| Sodium 473mg | 20% |
| Total Carbohydrates 3.6g | 1% |
| Sugars 2.3g | |
| Protein 2.2g | |
| Vitamin A 7% • | Vitamin C 1% |
| Calcium 5% • | Iron 2% |
| * Based on a 2000 calorie diet | |

Very high in vitamin B6

## HALLEE'S TRADITIONAL TURKEY GRAVY ❋ ⏱ ✡ 🍬 🦃

Turkey gravy is so vital to a turkey dinner. It is the final touch, and what could make or break the meal. It's also amazing poured over open faced turkey sandwiches. Don't be afraid of the seasonings – let the gravy be wonderful and full of flavor.

### INGREDIENTS:

2 cups plus $1/2$ cup Hallee's Heavenly Homemade Bird Broth ①, divided (See NOTES for variations)

$1/2$ to 2 tsp dried parsley

$1/2$ to 1 tsp ground sage

$1/4$ to $1/2$ tsp rosemary (to taste)

$1/4$ to $1/2$ tsp thyme (to taste)

-OR-

substitute Hallee's Inviting Italian Seasoning ① for the parsley, sage, rosemary, and thyme

$1/4$ to $1/2$ tsp garlic powder (to taste) (NOT garlic salt)

$1/4$ to $1/2$ tsp onion powder (to taste)

$1/2$ tsp fresh ground black pepper

Kosher or sea salt to taste

3 TBS organic cornstarch

### SUPPLIES:

saucepan or large skillet

measuring cups/spoons

small and medium bowls

whisk

### PREPARATION:

No special preparation is required

## DIRECTIONS:

Bring 2 cups of broth, pepper, sage, parsley, onion powder, and garlic powder to a boil. (Note: depending on the flavor of your broth, you may not need all of these seasonings – taste it and use your best judgment.)

In a small bowl, whisk $\frac{1}{2}$ cup cold broth (or water) with the cornstarch until smooth. Using a whisk, slowly pour the cornstarch mixture into the broth whisking as you pour until completely integrated.

As soon as it thickens, remove from heat (over cooking cornstarch will make it lose its thickening power.)

Salt to taste.

NUTRITION:

## Nutrition Facts

Serving Size 37 g

**Amount Per Serving**

| Calories 8 | Calories from Fat 0 |
|---|---|
| | **% Daily Value*** |
| **Total Fat** 0.0g | **0%** |
| *Trans* Fat 0.0g | |
| **Cholesterol** 0mg | **0%** |
| **Sodium** 171mg | **7%** |
| **Total Carbohydrates** 1.7g | **1%** |
| **Protein** 0.4g | |
| Vitamin A 0% • | Vitamin C 0% |
| Calcium 0% • | Iron 1% |
| * Based on a 2000 calorie diet | |

No saturated fat

No cholesterol

YIELD:

About 2 cups – or 8 servings

NOTES:

Taste as you season. So many variables make broths and gravies have different levels of seasoning. Sometimes you need more spices, sometimes you need less. Don't be wary of spicing up a bland gravy - your family will thank you for it.

ⓘ I have included the recipe for Hallee's Heavenly Homemade Bird Broth in this cookbook. If you don't have stock on ⬤and, but you are roasting a bird, you can use the juices you recover from your roasting bird in place of a broth. If neither is an option, use a good organic stock with low or no salt.

ⓘ You can find Hallee the Homemaker's instructions on how to roast the perfect turkey here:

http://www.halleethehomemaker.com/2010/11/roasting-the-perfect-turkey/

## WHY THE SUPER HERO?

## Invitation!

You may have noticed the armored character on the front cover of this cookbook. Throughout this book, you will see images of brightly colored warriors from the golden age of graphical stories. Heroic men and women are depicted in daring acts of selfless heroism.

These fictional heroes fight evil. They defend the defenseless. They save the world. Obviously, this is a parody cookbook, not a serious comic book or graphic novel. I appreciate the trappings of popular culture, especially when they lead to teachable moments.

After writing **Fifty Shades of Gravy**, I developed my writing mission statement: To prayerfully craft stories as modern day parables, uplift fellow believers, and minister to seekers in our fallen world.

As a society, we spend billions of dollars a year on television, movies, and books that glorify heroes and super heroes. Captain America, Batman, Spider-Man, Thor, Green Lantern, The Avengers, Superman, Iron Man 1, 2, and 3 - recent super hero movies that revolve around a man, or alien in the case of Superman, who is that one last hope for mankind - the one who can save us all.

AND THAT'S HOW I AM GOING TO SAVE THE WORLD.

POE

However, here in the real world, where men don't walk around in tights, flying armor, or winged helmets, we no longer need saving, because we've already been saved! In all of human history, there has only ever lived one man who had actual supernatural powers and that man used them to save the entire world.

> *"That if you confess with your mouth, "Jesus is Lord," and believe in your heart that God raised him from the dead, you will be saved." Romans 10:9*

Fictional super heroes do battle with fictional super villains, invading alien armies, artificial intelligences run amok, or just plain monsters. In other words, metaphors for real evil, demonic evil, that exists in the real world.

But if the very real Christ could have sat down to dinner with today's modern fictional super heroes, he would have explained that all they need to do is trust on Him, believe on Him, because Christ has already saved the entire world.

Saved from what?

From ourselves. From our sinful nature. God gave us a guide to righteousness in His commandments. When we break any of those commandments, we've sinned. We've broken God's law. When we break God's law, we are subject to His judgement, which is death. We are dead due to sin.

But Christ our Lord has already taken our punishment for that judgement. After the last supper, he suffered under Pilot and died on the cross for all of our sins. But on the third day after his death, he rose, conquering death and the grave. When we accept Him, love Him, become a follower of Him and His teachings, then we are saved from eternal death and granted eternal life.

That is what it means to be saved.

Maybe you think you don't need salvation. Maybe you think you're a good person and that's "good enough" so why do you need the real supernatural power that comes with accepting Christ? Is sin really that big of a deal? But in your heart of hearts, you feel that ache and you know there is more.

If you want to accept more, say this simple prayer.

*Dear God in heaven, I come to you in the name of Jesus. I acknowledge to You that I am a sinner, and I am sorry for my sins and the life that I have lived; I need your forgiveness.*

*I believe that your only begotten Son Jesus Christ shed His precious blood on the cross at Calvary and died for my sins, and I am now willing to turn from my sin.*

*You said in Your Holy Word, Romans 10:9 that if we confess the Lord our God and believe in our hearts that God raised Jesus from the dead, we shall be saved.*

*Right now I confess Jesus as the Lord of my soul. With my heart, I believe that*

*God raised Jesus from the dead. This very moment I accept Jesus Christ as my own personal Savior and according to His Word, right now I am saved.*

*Thank you Jesus for your unlimited grace which has saved me from my sins. I thank you Jesus that your grace never leads to license, but rather it always leads to repentance. Therefore Lord Jesus transform my life so that I may bring glory and honor to you alone and not to myself.*

*Thank you Jesus for dying for me and giving me eternal life. Amen.*

While it is certainly fun to munch popcorn and watch super powered fictional good guys save the planet one more time, the fact is that these modern stories are all just clever scripts, good actors, and awesome special effects. At the end of the day, they take off their costumes, wipe the makeup from their faces and they're just regular ol' sinners - like you and me - in need of the salvation that Christ offers.

# MEASUREMENTS & CONVERSIONS

| Liquid (Volume) Measurements (Approximate) | | | | | |
|---|---|---|---|---|---|
| 1/3 TBS | 1/6 fl oz | 1 tsp | 5 cc | 5 ml | |
| 1 TBS | 1/2 fl oz | 3 tsp | 15 cc | 15 ml | |
| 2 TBS | 1 fl oz | 1/8 cup | 6 tsp | 30 ml | |
| 1/4 cup | 2 fl oz | 4 TBS | 12 tsp | 59 ml | |
| 1/3 cup | 2 2/3 fl oz | 5 TBS & 1 tsp | 16 tsp | 79 ml | |
| 1/2 cup | 4 fl oz | 8 TBS | 24 tsp | 118 ml | |
| 2/3 cup | 5 1/3 fl oz | 10 TBS & 2 tsp | 32 tsp | 158 ml | |
| 3/4 cup | 6 fl oz | 12 TBS | 36 tsp | 177 ml | |
| 7/8 cup | 7 fl oz | 14 TBS | 42 tsp | 207 ml | |
| 1 cup | 8 fl oz | 1/2 pt | 16 TBS | 237 ml | |
| 1 pt | 16 fl oz | 1 pt | 32 TBS | 473 ml | |
| 2 cups | 16 fl oz | 1 pt | 32 TBS | 473 ml | |
| 2 pts | 32 fl oz | 1 qt | 1/4 gal | 946 ml | 0.946 l |
| 4 cups | 32 fl oz | 1 qt | 1/4 gal | 946 ml | |
| 8 pts | 1 gal/128 fl oz | 4 qts | 1 gal | 3785 ml | 3.78 l |
| 4 qts | 1 gal/128 fl oz | 8 pts | 1 gal | 3785 ml | 3.78 l |
| 1 l | 1.057 qts | | | 1000 ml | |
| 1 gal | qts | 128 fl oz | | 3785 ml | 3.78 l |

| Dry (Weight) Measurements (approx) | | |
|---|---|---|
| 1 oz | | 30 g  (28.35 g) |
| 2 oz | | 55 g |
| 3 oz | | 85 g |
| 4 oz | 1/4 lbs | 125 g |
| 8 oz | 1/2 lbs | 240 g |
| 12 oz | 3/4 lbs | 375 g |
| 16 oz | 1 lbs | 454 g |
| 32 oz | 2 lbs | 907 g |
| 1/4 lbs | 4 oz | 125 g |
| 1/2 lbs | 8 oz | 240 g |
| 3/4 lbs | 12 oz | 375 g |
| 1 lbs | 16 oz | 454 g |
| 2 lbs | 32 oz | 907 g |
| 1 k | 2.2 lbs/ 35.2 oz | 1000 g |

| (DRY) | 1 pt | 0.551 l |
|---|---|---|
| | 1 qt | 1.101 l |
| | 1 peck | 8.81 l |
| | 1 bushel | 35.25 l |

| (WEIGHT) | 1 oz | 28.35 g |
|---|---|---|
| | 1 lbs | 453.59 g |
| | 1 lbs | 0.454 kg |

| (LENGTH) | 1 in | 25.4 ml |
|---|---|---|
| | 1 in | 2.54 cm |
| | 1 ft | 304.8 ml |
| | 1 ft | 30.48 cm |
| | 1 yd | 914.4 ml |
| | 1 yd | 91.44 cm |

**HALLEE BRIDGEMAN** is a best-selling Christian author who writes action-packed romantic suspense focusing on true to life characters facing real world problems. Her work has been described as everything from refreshing to heart-stopping exciting.

An Army brat turned Floridian, Hallee finally settled in central Kentucky with her family so she could enjoy the beautiful changing seasons. She enjoys the roller-coaster ride thrills that life with a National Guard husband, a teenage daughter, and two elementary age sons delivers.

When not penning novels, she blogs about all things cooking and homemaking at **Hallee the Homemaker™** (www.halleethehomemaker.com). Her passion for cooking spurred her to launch a whole food, real food "Parody" cookbook series. In addition to nutritious, Biblically grounded recipes, readers will find that each cookbook also confronts some controversial aspect of secular pop culture.

Hallee loves coffee, campy action movies, and regular date nights with her husband. Above all else, she loves God with all her heart, soul, mind, and strength; has been redeemed by the blood of Christ; and relies on the presence of the Holy Spirit. She prays her work here on earth is a blessing to you and would love to hear from you. Contact information is on her website.

## COOKBOOKS BY HALLEE:

**Fifty Shades of Gravy**, a Christian gets Saucy

**The Walking Bread**, the Bread Will Rise

**Iron Skillet Man**, the Stark Truth about Pepper and Pots

## FICTION BOOKS BY HALLEE:

**Sapphire Ice**, book 1 of the Jewel Series

**Greater Than Rubies** (a novella inspired by the Jewel Series)

**Emerald Fire**, book 2 of the Jewel Series

**Topaz Heat**, book 3 of the Jewel Series

**Christmas Diamond** (a novella inspired by the Jewel Series)

**A Melody for James**, book 1 of the Song of Suspense Series

**An Aria for Nicholas**, book 2 of the Song of Suspense Series

**A Carol for Kent**, book 3 of the Song of Suspense Series (upcoming)

HOUSE OF BREAD

Better known as Bethlehem of Judea, the old Hebrew name *bêth lehem*, meaning "House of Bread," is known as the birthplace of King David and, above all, of Our Lord, Yeshua, known as Jesus of Nazareth. Thus, the "House of Bread" that is Bethlehem brought forth the Bread of Life that is our Savior.

The House of Bread Books™ imprint is pleased to publish healthy nutritious information in the form of cookbooks or informational pamphlets in order to better serve our community – the human race. We publish to reach every tribe and every nation for God has made of one blood all nations of men.

We pray that you enjoyed this fun attempt to redeem a recent secular phenomenon. Mostly, we pray that you come to know the joy and peace that is in serving Our Lord and Savior who is the King of kings, Lord of lords, and the Bread of Life.

Send inquiries to:

HOUSE OF BREAD BOOKS™
an imprint of: Olivia Kimbrell Press™
PO Box 4393
Winchester, KY 40392-4393

Or e-mail admin@oliviakimbrellpress.com

## FIFTY SHADES OF GRAVY

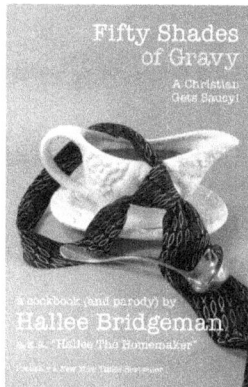

Hallee Bridgeman, A.K.A. "Hallee the Homemaker" rides the gravy train to triumph and hilarity with her première cookbook, revealing the secrets of the penultimate comfort food – gravy. Fifty Shades of Gravy "a Christian Gets Saucy!" is a cookbook wrapped in a parody surrounded by a comedy with a tongue firmly inserted into a cheek – but the recipes are deadly serious and may leave readers licking the gravy boat.

Her famous whole food, real food recipes bathe in luxuriant liquid comfort with recipes that are sure to captivate and enslave any audience. Hallee starts with stocks and broths and then explores every shade of gravy you can whip up. Some recipes are entire meals and some are simple sauces while still others are gravies served alongside a traditional holiday feast. There are meaty gravies, comfort food gravies, vegan gravies, gluten-free gravies, and even chocolate gravies! For any gravy question you were too ashamed to ask, this saucy Christian shares the answer.

Visit http://tinyurl.com/50gravyshades for more saucy information.

# THE WALKING BREAD

## The Bread Will Rise

Hallee Bridgeman, A.K.A. "Hallee the Homemaker" finds every grain of truth in her second whole food, real food cookbook with in-depth analysis and amazing recipes of yeast breads, quick breads, sourdoughs, and breads using grains other than wheat. The Walking Bread is a cookbook wrapped in a parody surrounded by a comedy with a tongue firmly inserted into a cheek – but the recipes are "dead serious" and may leave readers searching for all the tasty bread crumbs.

> "I am the bread of life. Your fathers ate the manna in the wilderness, and are dead. This is the bread which comes down from heaven, that one may eat of it and not die. I am the living bread which came down from heaven. If anyone eats of this bread, he will live forever; and the bread that I shall give is My flesh, which I shall give for the life of the world."
> John 6:48-51

Readers, bakers, homemakers, and cooks all over the world will find themselves slathering the good stuff atop the muffins or corn bread; speeding through the quick breads; and going ape of over the banana bread. These bread recipes are so good, so healthy, and so easy you will want to pass them down from generation to generation.

Visit http://tinyurl.com/walkingbread for more slices of information.

## HALLEE ONLINE

### Hallee Newsletter
http://tinyurl.com/HalleeNews/

Never miss updates about upcoming releases, book signings, personal appearances, or other events. Sign up for Hallee's monthly newsletter.

### Hallee the Homemaker blog
www.halleethehomemaker.com/

### Hallee Bridgeman, Novelist blog
www.bridgemanfamily.com/hallee/

# Index!

## C

## D

# H

# I

# K

## Z

UNAMBIGUOUS TABLE OF CONTENTS

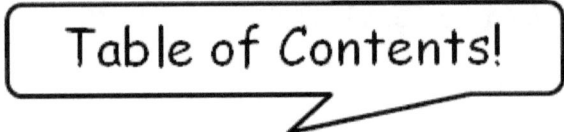

# Table of Contents!

www.ingramcontent.com/pod-product-compliance
Lightning Source LLC
La Vergne TN
LVHW051227080426
835513LV00016B/1444